Born in Chains

The Diary of an Angry Born-free

CLINTON CHAUKE

Born in Chains
The Diary of an Angry 'Born-free'

Jonathan Ball Publishers
Johannesburg & Cape Town

*This book is a memoir, but some names and identifying details have
been changed to protect the privacy of certain individuals. Likewise,
some events and conversations have been compressed or embellished.*

Originally published in South Africa in 2018 by
JONATHAN BALL PUBLISHERS
A division of Media24 (Pty) Ltd
PO Box 33977
Jeppestown
2043

ISBN 9781868428762
ebook ISBN 9781868428779

Twitter: www.twitter.com/JonathanBallPub
Facebook: www.facebook.com/JonathanBallPublishers
Blog: http://jonathanball.bookslive.co.za

Cover by Russell Starcke
Typesetting by Nazli Jacobs

Printed by **novus print**, a Novus Holdings company
Set in Lucida Std

For Kuhlula Ndlovu

Contents

Introduction

Often, in South Africa, it is the old and accomplished who share their stories. The youth are left to one side. This group of the old and accomplished often comments on the issues concerning the youth, but we hardly hear about these issues from the horse's mouth. I have decided to share my story as a young and proud black man living in South Africa. I have decided to share my experiences, and how I see the world, from this perspective. My story is not unique. It is similar to that of a lot of other young people in this country.

My fellow South Africans should read my story because I believe that, in it, we can all see ourselves. Its central message is to reject the 'born-free' label, which many people love to romanticise, forgetting its implications. Overall, I am telling my fellow South Africans, especially those who are young and black, that we are in a war! We are fighting for economic freedom. Politically, we are free, but economically, we are still far behind. I challenge my fellow young people to lift their thoughts, to question everything and to be courageous. After all, that is the essence of being young. To be young means to be idealistic. To be young means to be hyperactive.

To be young means to think without limits and never stop questioning the status quo.

In this book, I reflect on the past and critically analyse the present to save the future. Reflecting at the age of twenty-three may be very uncommon indeed, and may seem premature, but history has shown that it is the youth who have the capacity to move societies forward. It is the youth who often see the fractures in an unjust society. I hope you enjoy my story.

Chapter 1
Early life

I was born and bred in one of the poorest corners of South Africa. I am the product of labourers who grew up during the reign of one of the worst racial tyrannies the world has ever seen. The time when race was used to determine who was more, and less, human. The time when being black was like a disease.

Apartheid was the order of the day. Black people were already divided before apartheid was embraced by the government: when the National Party (NP) ascended to power after the country's general elections in 1948, they capitalised on the divisions that already existed between the country's different tribes.

When my mother was pregnant with me, South Africa conceived her democracy. It was ushered in by the first multiracial elections, which the African National Congress (ANC) won by a huge margin. The former Robben Island prisoner Nelson Mandela was sworn in as the first black president. Then, South Africa started to get confused.

My paternal grandfather was born during World War I in 1918, the same year that Nelson Mandela was born, far away from the corridors of power in Makrimani (ka-Buḓeli) village, west of the Rivhubye (Levubu) River in what is now Limpopo province. He would wake up every day dealing with the small matters of rural South Africa, always minding his own business, with his wife Tsatsawani Chauke and their five children – in order of birth, Mkhacani, Mbhazima, Mphephu, Mthavini and Jameson Chauke.

They resettled in Bevhula village after they were removed from the west side of Rivhubye, part of what is now called Ṱhohoyanḓou, the main centre of the Venda region, close to Nanḓoni, a key water source area. They planted mango, avocado and banana trees at their own home, known as ka-Dumazi.

In 1969, they were forcibly removed, like most Vatsonga, from areas that were to become the Republic of Venḓa. The Republic of Venḓa homeland was created as the Vhavenḓa Tribal Authority. Like Transkei, Ciskei and Bophuthatswana, this so-called 'republic' was another way in which the government perpetuated black division and white domination.

The Vhavenḓa gained power and coded '*Shumela Venḓa*' (Work for Venḓa) into their republic's coat of arms. This code symbolised the empowerment of Vhavenḓa, mostly through employment opportunities. Anyone who was not Muvenḓa – like my grandparents, who were Vatsonga – was not welcome and could not contribute to '*Shumela Venḓa*'. Many Vatsonga who had jobs in Louis Trichardt (now Makhado) were laid off to make way for Vhavenḓa.

The Vhavenḓa code led to serious tribalism against Vatsonga, who felt rejected and excluded. The tension be-

4

tween the two tribes still exists to this day – Vatsonga are demanding their own independent municipality in modern South Africa. My grandparents were transported with all their belongings, excluding their livestock, by huge trucks known as GGs (short for 'Government Garages') in 1969 and resettled on the eastern side of the Levubu River in Malamulele district.

Malamulele was the first district to be built in the former Tsonga homeland of Gazankulu, before the other six districts (Giyani, Nkowankowa, N'wa-Mitwa, Lulekani, Mhala and Hlanganani) were formed, their chief minister being Prof. Hudson William Edison Ntsan'wisi.

Not long after they arrived in Bevhula in 1970, my grandmother died in Tshilidzini Hospital, after suffering from respiratory problems. They put her on a stepladder, used as a casket, wrapped her in a blanket, and then buried her in the yard, since there was no cemetery in the village. My father had no real memories of his biological mother, Tsatsawani Chauke. He was mostly raised by his stepmother, Mjaji Chauke, whom my grandfather married after Tsatsawani's death.

When my grandparents arrived in Bevhula in 1969, the area was populated with wild animals such as elephant, lion and springbok. They used to burn firewood to drive the animals away. The European settlers would kill the elephants, wrap them in plastic bags and give them to my grandparents, who were staying in camping tents. They also gave them oranges and apples in an attempt to atone for the evil of removing them from the land they had occupied before. The wild animals remained at large, however, and in many instances they killed people – the western fence of the Kruger National Park was still open, being closed only in 1980.

The forced removal of Vatsonga, motivated by the racist laws of the time, disrupted the peaceful existence they had led in Makrimani. It reduced them to poverty and dependency on cheap wage labour in Johannesburg. My grandfather left his home *a ya xambila Joni* (and went to Johannesburg) to look for a job. He travelled by bicycle for over five hundred kilometres, taking rests in the bushes en route to Johannesburg. Upon arriving in Johannesburg, he stayed in the hostels of Jeppe and worked at a company called Sun Control.

He would visit my illiterate step-grandmother and his children very infrequently.

Unfortunately, he passed away when I was a year old. I am told that I look exactly like him. Everyone who knew him tells me I remind them of the old man. His name was Jackson. He named his son, my father, Jameson. I am told that my father wanted to name me Mackson to keep the rhythm going, but my mother refused.

My maternal grandfather, John 'JB' Baloyi, was born in 1920 in Sibasa, Venda. He later resettled in Potgietersrus (now Mokopane). He went to Johannesburg in 1950 to work as a miner and stayed in a hostel in Dube, Soweto, the township bordering Johannesburg's mining belt in the south.

My grandfather and other migrant workers who stayed in the hostels were later given houses according to their ethnic groups. In 1956, my grandfather got a house in the same township, house number 4185 Masungwini

Street, Chiawelo. *Chiawelo* is a Tshivenda word meaning 'place of rest'. It was where Vhavenda and Vatsonga were placed, since they had been neighbours in Limpopo. It was known in Xitsonga as *Tshiawelo tsha Vhavenda na Matshangani* (resting place for Vhavenda and Vatsonga).

In 1965, my grandfather met my grandmother, Lettie Ramadimetja Miyeza, who was staying in house number 5503 Nhliso Street, Orlando East – in the same township, Soweto. My grandmother was born there after her father, my great-grandfather, migrated from the ka-Xihosana section in Mdavula village in Malamulele.

My grandparents were blessed with their first child, Josephine, in 1969. And my mother, Khensani Baloyi, was born on 22 January 1972 in Baragwanath Hospital in Diepkloof, Soweto. In 1978, two years after the 1976 Soweto uprising, she started school at Hitekani Primary School, which was situated in front of their home in Chiawelo. It seems like the '76 student uprising had an effect on my mother's life growing up, because she didn't get that far in school; she dropped out in Standard 2 (Grade 4). She was not keen to open up to me about what really happened.

But, when my mother described her father, her face would quickly change. I could see that she was filled with anger. She highlighted that he was a very strict man. JB hated many types of people – those who were too slow or too fast, those who laughed too much and those who didn't laugh at all – almost everyone. It was because of this characteristic that many didn't enjoy his company.

7

When my grandparents migrated to Johannesburg, the impression was that a man had to go to Johannesburg and look for a job – this was a systematic setup by the apartheid government, which also made things so hard at school that the only solution was to quit and settle for the status quo.

Bantu education was, in effect, designed primarily to train black people for, and adapt them to, apartheid society. Hendrik Verwoerd, the policy's mastermind, said in a speech in 1954 that 'there is no place for [the African] in the European community above the level of certain forms of labour . . . it is of no avail for him to receive a training which has as its aim absorption in the European community . . .'. This meant that education played a crucial role in the apartheid system.

My grandparents and my parents must have been brainwashed by Verwoerd's statement, because all I heard while growing up was, '*U kula nwananga, u ta tirhela valungu* (Grow up, my son, so you can work for the white people).' Growing up, I didn't have a problem with these remarks – I was raised in an environment where white people were idolised and every good thing was attributed to *valungu* (white people). Today, Verwoerd's policies and statements disturb me very deeply and I made a vow that his words shall never be true of me.

What Verwoerd implied was that blacks like my grandfather could only work as labourers, general workers and servants. They could only stay in the homelands like Gazankulu, where they had restricted urban access, unless they were going to work in these kinds of jobs.

Verwoerd concluded that 'blacks must be taught from an early age that equality with Europeans is not for them'.

Indeed, they were taught that way. They got inferior education, learning in Afrikaans, a language that was, in effect, an instrument of oppression. In 1974, when Afrikaans and English were made compulsory as media of instruction, the students began to prepare themselves. The Black Consciousness Movement (BCM), led by Steve Biko, raised the political conscience of many students. On 16 June 1976, when the students took to the streets of Soweto and peacefully protested against the government's order, my mother was just four years old.

When my mother was eleven years old, my grandparents divorced. My grandmother moved away from her home in Chiawelo with her two children. She went to stay in the squatter camp in Mofolo, in the same township, Soweto. The land of the squatter camp was owned by Chief Tshabalala and was called after his clan name, Mshengu. While staying in Mshenguville, my grandmother met my aunt, Mthavini Chauke, who was staying with her family together with my father, in shack number 2388 Mshenguville, in Mofolo next to Dube.

My father had dropped out of Nkandziyi Primary School in Bevhula in 1981 when he was in Standard 5 (Grade 7). He had gone to look for a job in Johannesburg, where he stayed with his sister. He was a typical village boy who had grown up herding cattle and goats in the village of Bevhula. In 1981, the time when my father migrated to Johannesburg, nobody valued education.

9

My grandmother stayed in shack number 2389 Mshenguville, and became my aunt's neighbour. They were also colleagues in the sense that they were both street hawkers in Eyethu in Mofolo. My aunt sold herbs and my grandmother sold maize meal, tomatoes and onions to make ends meet.

By 1983, my grandmother had moved on to her second marriage. She went to Limpopo and got a new stead in Shirley village with her new husband. She had six more children: Nancy, Conny, Pertunia, Basani, Godfrey and Kulani, my aunts and uncles. My mother was left with her elder sister, Josephine, in Mshenguville. My grandmother moved back and forth between what is now Gauteng and Limpopo. She was quite a traveller, just like her mom – my great-grandmother – who had died after a short illness after visiting her brother at house number 81 Makuruntsi Street in Saulsville. She was buried at the Ten Morgan cemetery in Atteridgeville, the township in which I would later be born.

My mom and her sister continued with my grandmother's street hawking business in Eyethu. Through being acquainted with my aunt, my mother fell in love with my father when she was sixteen, in 1988. My father was working as a gardener. By the standards of those days, he was doing very well. My mother felt lonely and rejected after being left by her mother, and saw an escape from poverty in my father. My father was a last-born and a spoilt brat: his father, Jackson, would often travel from Jeppe to visit his children in Mshenguville and give my father some money.

My mother was an outspoken and impressive young girl. She smiled genuinely and laughed out loud, really hard. My father told me that she was a lover of people, but that, if you crossed a line, she was not afraid to put you back in your place really quickly. Men and women feared her for that.

My father took the daring step of approaching her. I could still see the love in my father's eyes when he explained how they started dating. '*Mhana wena a a ri na nkani, mara loko ani vona, a a dzika* (Your mother was very stubborn, but when she saw me, she would be calm).' They dated for a year and got married traditionally. My father paid lobola and they stayed briefly together in Bevhula village, my father's home.

In the meantime, the people in Mshenguville had been moved to different places. My aunt's family was moved to Orange Farm in the Vaal, where she still stays to this day. My aunt Josephine moved to Shirley village in Limpopo and built her own house, not far away from my grandmother's house. My grandmother's shack was moved to the old mining town of Durban Deep in Roodepoort, Johannesburg. She occupied the house until her death in 2016. With the prospect of new love and an ambition to stay in what is now Gauteng, my parents returned to where they had met, but they couldn't go back to Soweto because of these removals. They went to my father's brother, Abel Bilankulu, who owned a house in Pretoria.

Abel's mother and my father's mother were blood sisters. Abel had left the homelands earlier to stay in

Saulsville as a tenant while working as a truck driver for Transnet. When the owners of house number 106 Mackaya Street had decided to sell it, Abel had seized the moment and bought the house. He stayed there with his wife, Maria Bilankulu, and their five children – Cynthia, Percy, Marcia, Precious and Direction. When my parents joined them, it was one big family. They stayed in the back room of the four-room brick house together with some tenants that my uncle had secured.

By this time, my father was working as a driver for the Coca-Cola Company. Any family that had been in Saulsville for long enough to own the home they lived in were considered among the township 'top dogs'. It didn't matter that they had to rent out rooms to make ends meet, like my uncle did. Those who were born in Saulsville looked down upon those who had recently migrated there from Limpopo, like my family had. In those days, people who could be employed as teachers or policemen also considered themselves Saulsville 'top dogs'.

In 1991, my parents were blessed with a baby girl, my oldest sister. This was a special child, and they were very happy; they gave her a Xitsonga name – Tsakani, meaning 'happiness.' My second sister was born in 1993. She was also given a Xitsonga name – Akani, meaning 'to build'.

Shortly after Akani, I was born on Thursday 22 September 1994. I was also given a Xitsonga name – Wisani, meaning 'to rest'. It made sense that they named me this, because I was my parents' third and last born. So, after me, they rested indeed. My father was a dynamic man who loved politics. After being reprimanded about calling me Mackson, he gave me the second name of Clinton after the then President of United States of America, Bill Clinton. He believed that I, too, would be president someday. What an ambitious man!

Both my parents were dark in complexion, and their complexion was combined in me. I was the darkest child in our family. Out in the world later on, in Pretoria and Johannesburg, I was among the children who felt cursed to be dark-complexioned – it afforded some kind of status to be light in complexion. I learnt to hate every bone that was in me. My two sisters were fairly light in complexion, lighter than our parents. That always bothered me; because I was dark, society regarded me as ugly automatically.

Many black people were made to believe the white man's brainwashing, subconsciously favouring their light children as a result. My fellow black people instinctively treated lighter children better than us dark ones. The belief that the light-skinned children were better because they were nearer to being white came directly from apartheid.

My father was very lenient towards all his children. I don't remember him laying a hand on any of us. My mother is the one who would give us the whippings of our lives – especially me, because I was very naughty. She was very forgiving of Tsakani, a peaceful child who would never hurt a fly. As for me and Akani, we fought savagely as if we were monkeys in the wild.

I always disrespected Akani, and my mother always punished me for it. The main disrespect started very early. In Xitsonga culture, when you refer to someone who is your elder, you should always use a form of address that shows your respect, but I never called Akani *sesi Akani* (sister Akani). My mother would ask me, '*I mani loyi?* (Who is this?)' I would reply, '*I Akani* (It's Akani).' Then she would take out a belt and whip me. Once I was crying very hard, she would pause and ask again: '*I mani loyi?*' This time, I would say, '*I sesi Akani* (It's sister Akani).' She would whip me even harder then, saying, '*Se ni ku bela ku waswitiva ku I sesi wa wena* (Now I'm beating you because you know it's your sister).'

At this time, my father would intervene and say, '*Hey, unga ni dlayeli nwana wena* (Hey, don't kill my child).' Only then would my mother leave me alone. I loved my father for this. When I was with him, I did what I wanted and got away with it, while my mother never allowed any misbehaviour to go unpunished.

Even though my parents were married traditionally, my mother never changed her surname – they did not have a white wedding or go to Home Affairs to change her surname. And this, indeed, is how we do it in my Xitsonga culture. So, my mother remained Khensani Baloyi. But, according to European or Western norms, this meant that my sisters and I were bastards. Growing up, my schoolmates constantly reminded me about this – that I was a little bastard!

We were all born in Kalafong Hospital in Atteridge-ville, a township that was named after Myrtle Patricia Atteridge. Mrs Atteridge was the chairperson of the Pretoria City Council's Committee for Non-European Affairs in the 1930s. She was determined to improve the horrible conditions of the black people living in Lady Selbourne and Marabastad, near the city centre. They lacked food, proper sanitation and good housing.

Mrs Atteridge advocated better living conditions for these people until they were removed, in 1939, to Atteridgeville, which was established in that year to accommodate them. The township was extended to Saulsville, where my family stayed. Saulsville was planned as a residential area for whites, but was then bought by the city council, chaired by Mrs Atteridge, as an extension of Atteridgeville.

Families from Lady Selbourne were moved to Saulsville and families from Marabastad were moved to Atteridgeville – a name that the black people themselves suggested. It was originally intended to be called Motsemogolo ('big family') because it was a multicultural community, but they saw it fit to call it Atteridgeville, honouring Mrs Atteridge, who, in their eyes, was their Moses as she had taken them from captivity and brought them to a little Canaan.

The two townships, collectively, are also known as Phelindaba. This name was derived from two Xhosa words – *phelile (*meaning 'finished') and *indaba* (meaning 'discussion'). Phelindaba is translated, then, as 'end of discussion' – the end of the discussion about the people leaving their terrible living conditions and resettling in the township.

The township was connected by train to Pretoria's CBD. It was surrounded by Laudium to the north, the Proclamation Hills that proclaimed from the west, Lotus Gardens that blossomed in the south, and Saulsville, which extended Atteridgeville, to the east. The N4 route from Rustenburg marched in parallel with Church Street all the way to the CBD, which was ten kilometres away.

In Phelindaba, there were many sections, formed according to the tribes of the people who lived in them. We had Black Rock, which was mostly Bapedi, in the west. Ten Morgan was mostly Basotho in the north. Matebeleng was dominated by the Ndebele tribe in the centre. Selbourne Side, also known as Sabona, was dominated by Vatsonga and Vhavenda in the east. This is where we stayed. If you visited the township on a Saturday afternoon, you would think you were in a township somewhere in Malamulele. You would hear the music of Penny Penny from the middle-aged people, while the old people would still be hung up on Thomas Chauke. From the 'top dogs' you would often hear *bacadi* music drifting from speakers in the distance. This type of music had a beat similar to that of house music, but was mostly sung in Xitsonga. You would never know the artist's name; all you would know was that it was 'track 7'. When the 'top dogs' felt nostalgic, they listened to the old beats of kwaito. The cheese boys and cheese girls listened to American hip-hop and R&B. You could easily tell that they were very much influenced, just by the way they spoke, dressed and walked.

Oud Stad was dominated mostly by Batswana in the south. Kalafong Hospital, where I was born, was situated in the Oud Stad section. Bokgoni Technical Secondary

School, Holy Trinity Secondary, the Shell garage, Moroe Park and the Kalafong train station formed a complex at the Church Street entrance to Atteridgeville from the Pretoria CBD.

From Kalafong Hospital to the Union Buildings was a twenty-minute drive (fourteen kilometres) via the N4. The Union Buildings is the equivalent of the White House in America, the official seat of government and home to the offices of the president. I found it ironic that I was born a twenty-minute drive from the spot where Nelson Mandela was inaugurated in 1994.

I only realised later that I was, in fact, born close to the corridors of power – but far away from the reality of power.

Chapter 2

My home is a shack

Our family stayed briefly in Selbourne Side after I was born; my father wanted to find a place he could call his own. When I was three years old, he decided to move our family out of my uncle's four-roomed house in Saulsville. We moved to the newly formed squatter camp in Atteridgeville called Mshongo, in Phomolong section.

The area was part of what had been an old World War II ammunition dump, fifty years before the settlement of the first dwellers in Jeffsville section. It was cleaned up by bomb experts from the South African National Defence Force. People were advised not to erect their shacks in the area, because the ground there was very unstable. But, due to economic pressure and the lack of housing, they erected their shacks anyway; one section close to our section was called Siyahlala Nge Nkani, a Zulu phrase meaning 'we stay by force'.

My father erected a one-roomed shack on a plot allocated as JJ41 Phomolong using scrap wooden planks and asbestos plates. He used aluminium zinc for roofing. Our shack had no windows. On the floor, he put a mat as a carpet. In the early days, we would frequently find snakes under the mat.

Our house looked like most of the houses that were closely packed around it. It looked very old and rusted. The ones who had money were the ones who could paint their shacks. After building the shack, my father dug a hole and built a pit toilet not far away from it.

While my father was digging, a time bomb would be quietly ticking somewhere under the ground. Some bombs were found, usually after mudslides in the area. Others were found randomly around the place. Some were exposed when the squatters chopped firewood outside; whole families would be destroyed.

A task group of professionals was formed. My parents were constantly educated about the risk and asked to report any new finds to the police. The army explosives experts were often called in to remove the bombs. The squatters would often find mortars. The bombs would still contain their charge, but the noses and fuses would have been removed. Family friends Matimba Maphapha and Mbhoni Chavalala fell victim to an explosion while trying to pick up a mortar in Mshongo. Mbhoni lost the palm of one of his hands; Matimba fled unharmed.

Bra Peter was our neighbour on the left who had come from Mokopane. Bra Peter was a taxi driver. On the right, we had Blacky, who was working at the Coca-Cola Company. Everyone called him Blacky because of his complexion. Blacky didn't really care about anything. He lived alone, no wife or children. He consumed large amounts of alcohol.

Soon after we settled in Mshongo, Blacky almost burned down our home. His shack caught fire. It was very close to ours; the fire would have spread had it not been contained. Our shacks were very close to one another, creating an environment that promoted runaway fires and hindered access by firefighting trucks: the roads between the shacks were too narrow for them to enter the squatter camp. It then emerged that substance abuse was the cause of the fire at Blacky's home: he had kicked over a prama stove (a paraffin or Primus stove). Luckily, he was rescued and suffered only a few burns, adding to his blackness. We used firewood to cook, and sometimes *imbawula* (a coal stove). And, when we had money, we would use a Primus stove like Blacky.

Further along to our right, we had Bakaniya. I didn't know his real name. He was a huge fan of the Premier Soccer League club Orlando Pirates (the Buccaneers). So, everyone called him Bakaniya. Since I was still very young, Bakaniya called me Mkhalele, the name of a very dark-skinned Orlando Pirates striker, Helman Mkhalele. I was a very restless little boy, I am told. I would run around our untarred road causing all sorts of trouble. I ran so fast that Caster Semenya would have been proud, I am told.

Opposite Bakaniya was another die-hard Pirates fan called Samuel Skhosana. We called him Bra Sam. He had come from KwaNdebele.

Opposite us to the front was Moses Phala, who had come from Limpopo. Mr Phala sold sweets and chips before becoming a prophet for the Zion Christian Church (ZCC). Mr Phala's shack was inside a cave that was presumed to have been created by a bomb explosion. We called his home *a nghojini* (in the cave).

Opposite us to the back was a granny. We called her Kokwane Va Le Bush. She came from Bushbuckridge and was the only person who spoke Xitsonga in our area, so we got along with her family. Kokwane Va Le Bush's family was big. The family members shared rooms in the kind of squalor that would make you vomit.

Next to Kokwane Va Le Bush was the Mugwedi family. They had come from Venda. They built a brick house, and were consequently considered among the rich people of Mshongo. Their son, Mbuyelo Mugwedi, would later become my friend.

During those days, I still remember calling my parents when the truck that used to sell water would approach our house. I did the same thing when I heard the siren of the ice cream truck approaching. I remember that my father liked to lift me up. I would get strange stomach sensations when he did.

Our home was situated on a hill, about four hundred metres away from the taxi rank in Maunde Street, Atteridgeville's longest street. That is where we would take a taxi to town.

We lived next to Atteridgeville Extension 7. The extension of the township was part of the new government's Reconstruction and Development Programme (RDP). When we moved to Mshongo, my parents immediately applied for an RDP house. This was in early 1998; they have been waiting for the government to provide them with a better home ever since. I don't know how the government decides who gets a house. My parents have been on the waiting list all this time, but have never

21

heard a thing. Some people, like Blacky, would complain that they earned too much to qualify for free government housing, but not enough to buy their own house.

A house was a basic need for anyone staying in Mshongo. A walk through Mshongo would show conditions that no human being should ever have to live in – conditions that went against our Bill of Rights. However, the story of my community was nothing unique; it was a nightmare that was lived in many other ignored places, all across the country. Our squatter camp was similar to Motsoaledi in Diepkloof, Soweto, or Stjwetla in Alexandra, or Winnie Mandela in Tembisa, or Phomolong in Mamelodi, or Enkanini in Khayelitsha, or Marry Me in Soshanguve, or Emhlabeni in Umlazi.

Crime was rife during those days in Mshongo. The dangerous conditions that had been forced on us led to unnecessary tragedy and heartbreak: we would constantly lose our loved ones in those bad conditions.

We only stayed briefly in Mshongo, however, due to the conflict between my parents. I still have memories of the friction between my father and mother. Sometimes, it would even get physical. It may have had something to do with my father's laziness: time and again, he would quit his job without a valid reason. His drinking tendencies also got the better of him. My mother was very sharp. Every time she called him out, he would grab her. When she could not take it any longer, she decided to leave him.

Chapter 3

Monkeys are my friends

When my parents' feuding reached a climax and they separated, my mother became known as *xivuya*, a Xitsonga term given to a woman whose marriage has failed. She took all her children and went to her mother's homestead in Shirley village, which was on an isolated farm neighbouring Waterval township to the west and Mbhokota village to the east. It was the land of the Njhakanjhaka Traditional Authority.

Shirley was divided into sections called *miganga*. The section above Waterval township was called Amudzwiriti. It was at the western entrance of the village, where Shirley Primary School was situated. The section below the mountain was called Axigodini. My aunt Josephine stayed in Axigodini, with her Mozambican husband and their children Amukelani, Oscar, Rirhandzu and Pfumelani – not far away from Vonani Bila's home. Mr Bila is a writer.

The section on top of the mountain and above Mbhokota village was called Axitasini. That is where we stayed, on the steep mountaintop. The soil's texture was soft and it was very red. When it rained, it would be disastrous. When I was very young, I used to think that, if I were to fall, I would roll all the way down the mountain. Luckily, I later learnt about gravity at school. Damn education, ruined my imagination!

The section next to Axitasini on a small hill was called Akanani. Akanani was more of a recreational centre and provided jobs for the locals. My uncle Kulani used to have a friend who stayed in Akanani. The guy would yell at Kulani, who would respond. They made a lot of noise.

Akanani faced Axitasini. The two were separated by a tarred road, the R578, which transported people from ka-Magoro, ka-Bungeni, ka-Mbhokota and other small villages to the shopping complex in Elim, which was roughly two kilometres from Shirley.

Our homestead was the first stead when you entered Shirley from the Akanani entrance. There was a water-pump station in the middle of a grassless soccer field, and H.S. Phillips Secondary School. When you stood in the back yard of H.S. Phillips Secondary, it was possible to see over ten small villages down the mountain.

Immediately after passing the soccer grounds, you would walk into our home, ka-Baloyi Ka Mhani Lettie (Lettie Baloyi's home). The neighbouring steads were ka-Baloyi Ka Vo Tlangi (Tlangi Baloyi's home) on the right, and ka-Xikava on the left. Mr Xikava was a policeman in Malamulele. Across from us at the back was ka-Mashamba. On the weekends, the villagers would gather at the soccer field in front of our home to support the local team, Matlharhi FC, a team my uncles used to play for. The steads were scattered all over the mountain.

Shirley village sat at the front of the Rivolwa Mountain.

Chavani village called the other side of the mountain its home. Vatsonga Cultural Village sat on top of Rivolwa Mountain, created to preserve the history of Vatsonga, which was under attack from some European influencers. The government helped build this remarkable place.

When my grandmother went back to Johannesburg, my mother became the eldest person in our home – the responsible person in the family. My other aunt, Nancy, was also staying with us – together with her two children, Nyeleti and Vutivi. It was a very big family. There were three houses in our homestead. One was a very big rondavel house, called N'winyi Wa Muti (home owner) All the women slept in this house. Across from it was another rondavel house in which my uncles slept. Between the rondavels, we had a small shack that we used as a kitchen. Our yard was not fenced. At night, we would sit around the fire, playing and teasing one another.

In the morning, when the guys went to school, my mom would wake up and sweep the yard, then prepare the food for the guys. She would usually cook pap and some vegetables from her garden on a big, size-eight three-legged pot. Her favourite vegetable was called *mxiji*. During lunch breaks, my aunts and uncles would come home to eat since their school was very close to our home. My sisters and cousins would be given lunchboxes to take to school in the mornings – at Shirley Primary School, they didn't allow the kids to leave during break-time, unlike H.S. Phillips.

In January 2000, my mother took me and my cousin

Oscar to enrol at Shirley Primary School. We were rejected: '*Va dyiwa hi lembe vana lava mhani* (These kids are one year behind, ma'am),' the school principal, Mr Zinjhiva, said to my mother. Shirley Primary admitted pupils who were six years old, or who were five years old but had been born before June. I was born in September and Oscar was born in June, so we were ultimately rejected on those grounds. I remember being ready, wearing my uniform, when my dream of going to school was shattered. Akani and Tsakani were enrolled at Shirley Primary; I would wake up every day with no prospects for the future. This was very bad for a young man. I was bored; when the others went to school, I would play with my cousin Vutivi, and Oscar would often visit us from Axigodini.

Noticing our boredom at home, my mother assigned jobs to me and Oscar: '*Oscar na Clili, mi rindza tinkawu ku ti nga dyi mavele amasinwini* (Oscar and Clili, keep the monkeys from entering the garden),' she would say. The vervet monkeys would often invade our home. My mom had planted maize meal and *mihlanta* (sweet potatoes), and there were mango, avocado and banana trees in our yard. I was very young, and thought it was normal for monkeys to live around people. We would always watch for the monkeys. When they came into the garden, we would pick up *magavadi* (compacted soil), since there were few rocks, and throw it at them. I thought it was just a game we played with them – my logic was that, when they saw us, they would run away.

When the older guys came home from school, we would

26

be relieved of our duties. We would then go and provoke the monkeys at the village's entrance at Akanani, where there were very tall trees known as *midlamethi*. The monkeys were very many in that part of the village; you would often find them brachiating there. Sometimes, they would attack the villagers arriving home from the shopping centre in Elim. They usually attacked people who were carrying fruits or vegetables.

They once ambushed my uncle Godfrey. They took his bananas. When he got home, everyone laughed at him. Soon after that incident, one of them attacked Oscar while we were throwing stones at them. I will never forget that day: he threw a stone at one in front of him and, from behind him, one jumped on top of him then ran away, leaving him lying on the ground. Upon seeing what had happened, I followed the monkey, running away from Oscar and moving towards the soccer grounds.

'*He Clinton,* why *uni siya?* (Hey Clinton, why are you leaving me behind?)' he cried.

Hearing about my uncle Godfrey being attacked, and then seeing my cousin Oscar getting attacked, made me realise that the monkeys had never attacked me. I had a good record; using this logic, I concluded that the monkeys were my friends.

At home, the girls were responsible for cooking and for fetching water from the tap, which was very close to our home. My uncle Kulani would usually go to soccer practice at the dusty field. And Godfrey would usually swim in the village's dam, which was next to Rivolwa Mountain. The name of the dam was Dombani. We were instructed not to go near Dombani dam under any circumstances: there had been disastrous floods in February and March of that year. Heavy rainfall had lasted for five weeks, leaving many people homeless; the Limpopo River had grown to twice its normal level.

Soon after the disaster had started, Chief Njhakanjhaka summoned the villagers to a meeting at Hubyeni at Rivoni, a small village where the SABC presenter Rhulani Baloyi was born. Rivoni was very close to Shirley. The meeting was held at the Njhakanjhaka Traditional Authority offices – close to the Rivoni School for the Blind, which Ms Baloyi had attended. The chief gave the villagers some guidelines about evacuation procedures.

Shirley was mountainous. So, those of us who stayed in Axitasini were safe, unlike those in Axigodini, who lived on the floodplain at the foot of the mountain. Community members built levees and terraces – only if these proved inadequate would they be willing to move to a place of safety. Some families from Axigodini were evacuated to Axitasini.

My aunt Josephine evacuated during the disaster time and came to stay with us. As the floods continued, our home started to be affected as well. My uncle covered N'winyi Wa Muti with plastic sails to protect it – inside the house was a double bed and mirror, bought from Ellerines on credit. (I know this for sure, because it was later repossessed. Even though I was still young, I still remember the embarrassment when the bakkie came to take the bed and *xipilikasi*, or mirror, back.) My uncle also covered his house with plastic sheeting. My mother,

28

a religious woman, asked the whole family to pray that the rain would stop.

But the plastic tarpaulins were not adequate. I remember my mom saying, '*N'winyi Wa Muti wa mbindzimuka* (The house is crashing down).' Indeed, it was. The mud house started losing its plaster; we watched it falling down slowly. By the time the rain stopped, the house had collapsed. No one was injured, though.

We were better off than the people in Mozambique, however. We heard on Munghana Lonene FM, an SABC radio station, that the floods in Maputo, six hundred kilometres away, were severe. People were forced out of their homes, and had to climb onto roofs and into trees in the hope of being rescued. One woman was even forced to give birth in a tree. Luckily, she was saved by the air force.

For the duration of our stay in Elim, my father only visited us once. He came with his friend Solly Mathevani, who owned a Toyota Cressida. On the day he left, I cried to go back with him to Atteridgeville. And I did – my father insisted, and saw fit to take me back with him. This was obviously a big moment in my childhood. I had been surrounded by many people up to now, but my father was not in their midst. I missed him a lot. At the end of the day, a child needs both parents.

My father took me to our cousin, who stayed very close to where he was staying. I only realised later that male parents are unable to look after children on their own. He was working as a taxi driver, driving a Toyota E20. I don't remember much about this time, because I was still very young, but I am told that I was not treated well at my cousin's place – that I was treated like a slave. I am told that my grandmother, who was staying in Roodepoort, rescued me from the Egypt-like captivity I found myself in. She travelled from Johannesburg to Pretoria, fetched me, then proceeded to her homestead in Elim, where she dropped me off with the words, '*Nwana nwananga a nge hlupheki na ha hanya* (My grandson will not struggle while I am still alive).'

My father's taking me to Pretoria symbolised the tension between my parents. As a small child, I thought it was normal for parents to fight all the time. In the end, however, my parents managed to iron out their differences. We moved back to my father's homestead in Bevhula village, rejoining forces with him when he came back from Pretoria.

Chapter 4

The Kruger National Park, my new home

It was 2001 when my mother, together with Akani and Tsakani, moved to my father's homestead in Bevhula. By this time, we had moved three times since I was born. I started school at Nkandziyi Primary School the same year. This is the home where I started to grow up and remember things.

Bevhula formed part of the farm called Ntlhaveni. Ntlhaveni consisted of small villages – Block A ka-Mashobye, Block B ka-Nkavele, Block C ka-Makhuvele, Block D ka-Hlungwani, Block E ka-Magona, Block F ka-Nghomunghomu, Block G ka-Bevhula, Block H ka-Makahlule, Block I ka-Makuleke and Block J eMabiligwe.

All these villages belonged to *tihosi* (chiefs). Each chief had a village under his ownership. The Bevhula chief's grandson, the musician Kenny Bevhula, was the most popular person among the Xitsonga-speaking people of South Africa.

Small rivers separated the village from ka-Mashobye to the south, from ka-Makhuvele to the east, and from ka-Makahlule to the west; to the north, one separated the village from the ten-metre-high border fence. These small rivers joined together strategically and fed into the

31

Levubu River, which marched all the way to the Limpopo River.

Bevhula was twenty kilometres away from the town of Malamulele. It was two villages away from Salema village, the home of the legendary Xitsonga artist Dr Thomas Chauke. It was the last village before the border fence that separated South Africa from Mozambique. It was just a little bit shy, and lay to the south of the road that led to the Phunda Maria gate (a direct entrance to the Kruger National Park). When wild animals such as lions and elephants escaped from the Kruger National Park, their first destination was Bevhula. The landscapes of Bevhula were so beautiful; were the region not so poor, it could have been the best recreational area in South Africa. There were a lot of hills, but no mountains like Rivolwa. The soil structure was mainly sandy grey soil (*ntlhava*); this is the reason the farm was called eNtlhaveni.

The village was also divided into *miganga* (sections), as in Shirley. My father was still staying at the homestead where he had been brought up by his stepmother, in a section known as Axikhulu – the original homesteads – in the centre of the village. Most of the homes were known by the name of the old man in the house. Our home was known as ka-Jikiseni (Jackson's home); on the left was ka-Mbarhi (Barry's home); on the right, ka-Mhani Johanah (Johanah's home); in front and opposite, ka-Gija (Gija's home); and next to ka-Gija was ka-Kokwane N'wa-Xilele (Granny N'wa-Xilele). All these homes had a kraal of cattle. We didn't have cows at our home, because there was no boy to herd them. My step-grandmother only had goats.

I would always go to Rivoningo and Matlharhi at ka-Kokwane N'wa-Xilele, who were herding. I would even go with them to *dibini* (the dip). Here, the cows would be dipped into a pool of Jeyes Fluid to clear themselves of parasites and diseases. We would also eat *xithuvi* (cooked milk) together.

The village had extended to the north. This section was called Anyusitandi Ya Le Masirheni (new homesteads towards the cemetery). And there was Anyusitandi Ya Le Danwini (new homesteads towards the dam) in the south.

My step-grandmother, Mjaji Chauke, born in 1929, lived alone and did not have children. She was widowed when my grandfather passed away in 1995. She made a living by brewing and selling traditional beer called *umqombothi*.

She would wake up very early in the morning to mix equal quantities of *manjanja* (sorghum) with maize meal. She made a paste of this with boiling water in a huge plastic container called *diromu*. She would store the mixture in the dark corner of our kitchen for two or three days, depending on the temperature. When the mixture smelled a little fermented, she would boil water in a pot and add the paste slowly while stirring it continuously using a big stick called *dyi nkombe ledyi kulu*. Once it was cooked, it was called *madleke* and it was delicious, like mageu. During this time, she would serve us *madleke*. The final product would also be called *madleke* by the drinkers.

She would continue with the process by mixing the

madleke with cold water and mushing it up with her hands until it was drinking consistency. The success of the *umqombothi* depended on the magic of one's mixing hand. My grandmother was very gifted – she was not the only person in the village who made *umqombothi*, but she had more customers than her peers. Once she had mixed the *madleke* with cold water, she would add more *manjanja* to the mixture. She would place it back in the dark corner for about three days while it fermented. When *umqombothi* has fermented, it has a strong, bitter smell and little bubbles pop on the surface. Only after all these days would the *umqombothi* become available.

She would put up a long pole with a yellow jar on it to signal that the alcohol was ready. The village men would then say, '*Bya bava ka-Jikiseni* (The beer is available at Jackson's house).' She sold *umqombothi* at various prices, depending on the size of the serving, called *xikalo*. It was cheap – it ranged from R2 to R7. Once the yellow jar was put out, our home would be packed until the day the *umqombothi* finished.

She also had a little fridge and sold Castle Lager and Black Label for the village snobs who didn't drink *umqombothi*. Boti Harry was one of those snobs. He was a pensioner; by Bevhula standards, Boti Harry was a very rich man because he used to work in Johannesburg. Anyone in Bevhula who had been to Johannesburg also considered themselves to have made it in life.

Boti Harry would tell jokes for days. He also liked to tease people, especially those who drank *umqombothi*, as they were known as *bo-Mahlalela* (the lame ducks). He would tell them a bunch of stories from Johannesburg as they shared *umqombothi* from big clay jar or jug. It was considered disrespectful to drink *umqombothi* while standing or wearing a hat. They would sit in a circle around him as if he were a fire on a cold winter's morning. When I walked past them, he would pause and say, '*Jikiseni, tana la* (Jackson, come here),' then he would shake my hand and proceed to tell me how I reminded him of my grandfather – *a mi bihe ku fana* (he was ugly as you), he would say.

When we arrived in Bevhula, I noticed that there was a bit of tension between my step-grandmother and my mother. They did not see eye to eye. At times, they would even confront each other. My mother didn't like my grandmother's tendency to send me around. '*A hi hlonga nwana wa mina* (My son is not a slave),' she would say, and my grandmother would simply reply, '*Mafurha ya nwana i ku rhumiwa* (It is a child's duty to be sent).' I found their rivalry normal; no *makoti* (bride) has ever got along with her in-laws. I have never seen that happen anywhere.

The tension between my mom and step-grandmother escalated until my father decided to leave and build his own home. The new steads in the north and south of the village were formed by people like my father. They all came from Axikhulu; then, when they were older, they were supposed to leave and build their own home to symbolise the stage of maturity they had reached.

My father bought a new stead from the chief, Mzamani

Erick Ndlovu, at a price of R20, among the new steads towards the dam. He avoided the new steads towards the cemetery, because there were rumours that people saw ghosts in that area of the village. He began preparing to build. He started by removing the topsoil, clearing and levelling. He would wake up every day to form mud bricks, which we called *ku foroma*. He dug two trenches for circular foundations. After school, I would usually go and watch him use a pole in the centre of the circle with a string line to measure and mark out the radius of the rondavel.

He then started to build the houses. When he reached windowsill height, he set the window frames. Then, the two houses – which were about twelve metres in diameter and five metres tall, and had a single entry and exit point – stood without a roof for two months.

During the winter, my mom had woken up very early, before the sun, to go and cut dry grass for thatching. My father chopped down *timbalele* (flexible saplings) in preparation for building a roof. The construction crew, which included all my father's friends – Ndoza, Divava and Boti Eddie – came and helped my father put up a roof structure. The beams for the roof were attached to the rebar embedded in the lintel, or bondbeam, called *xihlungwani*. Then, they used the dry grass that my mother had collected by hand over many months for thatching. Thatching was probably the most laborious part of the entire project, but was the simplest: all it involved was placing the grass on top of the structure.

They plastered the houses. Then they painted them using a water paint known as *kalaka*. They painted one house with bright-blue *kalaka* and the other one with bright-green *kalaka*, the colours of Vatsonga Machangani, the Shangaan people of Vatsonga heritage. When the rondavels were built, my mother built *maguva* (small walls) to join the two houses. Then she put mud on the floor and floated the floor to make it smooth, which we called *ku ridela*. Finally, she got *vulongo* (bull manure) and decorated the floor. Our home was very beautiful.

We stayed with my step-grandmother for a year in Axikhulu. We moved into our new home, the two rondavel houses that my parents had built, in 2002. We used the blue house as a bedroom and the green house as *xitanga* (the kitchen). But, before we moved in, my mother called Pastor Hlungwani from Block C Zion Christian Church to pray for the new steads and drive out evil spirits. I remember Pastor Hlungwani burning some papers and sprinkling the whole yard with water and salt as we were preparing to move in.

In the bedroom rondavel was one double bed where my parents slept. We slept on the floor. I would always sleep in the middle, between my sisters. Even when we took photos, I would always be in the middle. There was a small carpet with glasses that were stored on it for visitors – we never used those glasses. The only time I made contact with them was when I broke them. I used to break a lot of the visitors' glasses. One day, as I broke a glass, my mom yelled, '*Clinton! Teka na letiya tinga laya henhla u fayetela na tona* (Clinton! You might as

37

well take the ones on top and break them too).' She said this while she was preparing a belt to whip me.

Our neighbour was Sesi Mihloti on the right. Behind Sesi Mihloti was Hahani Mavis. Just like in Mshongo, out back opposite us was a granny. We called her Kokwane Va Ka Hanyani. Kokwane Va Ka Hanyani had a house which had a veranda, which we called *yindlu ya ma zingi*. Any family that had *yindlu ya ma zingi* was automatically considered among the village's elite. Out front opposite us was ka-Macevele. Next to ka-Macevele was Happy's mother. She used to work at a tomato firm, ZZ2, and would always complain about being tired – *a matama-tisini ka tika* (it's tough at work), she would say. On our left side, there was nothing – we were the last stead in the village. Our neighbour on that side was *nsinya wa nkanyi* (a morula tree). During summer, we would have a treat. Some village grannies would often come and pick morula to make *byala bya vukanyi* (home-made morula beer). These grannies were the real competition for my grandmother in the brewing industry. Witnessing the beautiful African sunset from my home was the best thing ever. From our home, it was just morula trees, then there was about two hundred metres of bush just before the dam, which was further south towards Block C.

Just like in Shirley, my mother advised me not to go near the dam: '*Unga yi le danwini, kuna tingwenya* (Do not go to the dam, there are crocodiles).' During rainy seasons, hopeful villagers would pass our home to go fishing and, when the water levels dropped, they would simply use a big net to trap the fish in bulk. Two people would stand about six metres apart with big net. Then, they would dip it into the water and trap the fish in big numbers. The process was called *ku kukutla*. It was a dangerous process because the crocodiles would be out in full force.

In the new steads, we also had our own *nsimu* (garden) where we grew our own food. My step-grandmother had given us some chickens and chicks that we raised when we moved out. Akani had a good hand, for all her baby chicks grew to be edible chickens that would be slaughtered on special occasions or when we had visitors. My baby chicks never matured; I was still very young to be nursing young lives.

The chickens slept in the kitchen. In the centre of the kitchen was a fire where my mom used to cook food and behind the door was a three-legged pot that she used for cooking. We washed our hands in the same pot that had *makoko* (the remains of pap mixed with water) in it.

The chickens went to sleep very early, at about six. We would lock them in. At this time, we were using a small bush as a toilet. Then my father dug two holes. One was for building a pit toilet and the other was *tala* (where you bury ashes from the kitchen). Because the chickens went to sleep early, they woke up earlier than we did. When they crowed in the morning, they would wake us up. The chickens were our alarm; when the cock crowed, we would wake up and prepare to go to school. Since I was the youngest, I would wait for my sisters to bath, then my mother would bath me.

I wore black trousers, a white shirt and black shoes.

At Nkandziyi, they didn't really care about school uniforms. Some pupils came to school with their clothes from home. The teachers understood, because we were poor. Akani and Tsakani wore skirts that were pleated or a black dress called *dangara*. We used plastic bags to put our books in. My favourite was a Shoprite one. Akani's favourite was a Checkers one. Tsakani was fine with anything. A school bag was a luxury in those days.

Just like in the squatter camp in Atteridgeville, there was no electricity in our new home. But there, it was very different: it was safe. I figured out later that the reason the crime rate was so low in the village was because there was nothing to steal. Criminals steal when there is something worth stealing; in the village, everyone was poor.

In the village, I was afraid not of criminals, but of witchcraft. I was afraid of walking alone at night, because every day I would hear scary stories about the witchcraft that was taking place in the village. Almost every *gogo* (granny) in our village engaged in a strong magic called *vuloyi* (witchcraft) – especially those who went to church. They used their strong belief in magic for evil purposes, with the aim of harming the community. As a precautionary measure, we were told not to eat food from other homes or walk barefoot – if we ate from other homes, the food could poison us and if we walked barefoot, the witches could take the soil that had our footprints in it and use it to bewitch us, my mother said.

At Happy's house, they once caught a woman who was stuck in the yard. It was believed that she had been busy with the acts of witchcraft – we said *uxwerini*.

40

Happy's mother never spoke to the woman. The whole village went to see her, as she was struggling to get out. She only managed to leave when they started conversing with her.

During those years, we would wait for the moon, then we would go play outside at night with my sisters and their friends. We had mastered the science and art of the stars and the universe; we knew that the earth was round and not flat. We knew what different phases of the moon represented seasonally. My sisters hated playing with me. They always suggested that I go and play with the other boys and stop playing with girls – '*Famba huhwa na vo vanghana va wena* (Go and play with your friends).' We played games like touch: someone would touch you, then everyone would run away from you until you could touch someone yourself. My favourite game was *khuchukhuchu-america*. To play the game, we all held hands to form a line in single file, like a train. Then, two people who had given themselves names – say, Chips and Sweets – would join hands above their heads to form a bridge for the train to go under. This bridge was the train station. The train would move and we would sing, '*Khuchu-khuchu . . . America! Stimela sa bampa! America!*' It would pass through this station, and the last person in the line would be caught in the station. That person would have to choose between Chips and Sweets. If you chose Sweets, you would go and stand behind Sweets. We would do that until the last person had gone to stand behind either Chips or Sweets. Then, we would draw a line between Chips and Sweets. Sweets, with his or her people, would try to pull people from Chips over the line. The team that pulled all the people over to its side would win the game. We also played hide-and-seek.

My not-so-favourite moment was when we were done playing and I had to go back home to bath. I did not enjoy that part at all. Most of the time, my mother would have to call me: '*Clili riperini dyambu vuya kaya* (Clili, come back home, it's late).' My mother called me Clili. That's how she shortened 'Clinton'. If she yelled 'Clili', I knew everything was fine. But if she yelled my full name, I knew I was in trouble.

By mid-2002, we had settled very well into our new home. My mother was an early riser. She would wake up every day before sunrise to go to the forest to chop firewood for a huge stockpile, known as *xithope xa tihunyi*, outside our entrance. She would come back with a stack of wood balanced on one hand. The pile of wood stretched a few metres behind her and few metres in front of her.

I remember, when I was in Grade 1, my class teacher giving us an instruction to tell our parents that we had to come to school with one piece of firewood to contribute to the firewood that the women who ran the feeding scheme used. '*U byela* mistress *wa nwina ku va penga* (Tell your teacher that she is out of her mind),' my mother instructed me. I did exactly that. It caused a huge feud; my mother went to Mrs Macevele's home, which was in the village. They fixed their problems and excused me, because I was still very young.

But the order from our school's principal, Mr Mbhambho – who had taught my father – was followed. We

42

went to school with one piece of firewood every day. If you failed to do so, you would not get food from the feeding scheme. The scheme usually served us soup and bread, cooked on a huge three-legged pot using the fire-wood we had brought. On other days, we simply got soft porridge. We would take our own container to school to eat from. At breaktime, we would queue under a big willow tree in front of the school's administration block and get our food.

In the rainy season, the roads would flood and the bread truck would not be able to reach our village to deliver bread. '*Namuntlha a ku dyiwi, movha wa xinkwa awu nge fiki* (Today, there will be no school feeding – the bread truck could not get to our village),' the announce-ment would be made. This would force us to rely on the food our parents bought.

The feeding scheme was not accountable to the school governing body. My mom would often talk of food dis-appearing from school, and theft by the people who provided the food.

In Grade 2, my class teacher, who was a Muvenda lady, expelled me from her class for walking into class with my shoes on. I didn't attend her class for a month until my mother went to school to resolve the matter. Mrs Tshifu-laro's classroom was the cleanest, because she was strict: when we got to her class, we were supposed to take off our shoes. We were also required to take our own chairs to school, since there was a shortage of chairs.

The playing field of our school was covered in weeds. Our school was in such bad condition that, at any moment, the classrooms we were taught in could have collapsed. We shared two classrooms for all our lessons, which happened simultaneously: the other classrooms were so badly damaged that they were unusable. '*Nwina va ka A langutisani hala ivi va ka B mi langutisa le* (Grade 1 learners, look this way; Grade 2 learners, face that way),' Mrs Tshifularo would say, pointing in different directions in the classroom. It was very difficult for her to teach learners from different grades, all sitting in one small, dilapidated classroom. Added to that, we used pit toilets, although this was not a problem because we also used them at home.

One morning, while we were preparing to go to school, my mother came home terrified, without any firewood. '*Ni siyi tihunyi a nhoveni, ni vone nghala ivi ni tsutsuma* (I left the firewood in the bush after seeing a lion),' she explained. She was not first person to have made this allegation. Many villagers had said the same thing. This was during the time in 2002 when some animals from the Kruger National Park had escaped. Immediately after the news surfaced, Chief Erick Ndlovu called a meeting, known as *xivijo*. They discussed evacuation procedures and how to prevent attacks.

One afternoon, when I had just arrived home from school with Akani, I saw something beautiful that my eyes had never seen before: a giant elephant, walking with a small elephant. They were going to drink water at the dam, which was about two hundred metres from our home. I didn't know that what I was seeing was a potential threat to my life; my young mind failed to compre-hend the seriousness of the situation. I couldn't wait to change out of my school uniform and tell my friend Sergeant Maphapha, who stayed one block away from our home. As a child, I thought it was normal for people to live so close to wild animals.

A week later, it was found that the lions had killed cows in the nearby forest. The national park people ad-vised the villagers not to kill the animals, since that would be a criminal offence. The national park advocated more for animals' lives than people's lives. This was my earliest observation that the animals in this country were better cared for than the people. Fast forward to a de-cade later, in Bronkhorstspruit: I saw an old white man sitting in a bakkie, with his dog in the front seat and his black employee outside, on the back of the bakkie – an interesting indication of the inequalities that exist be-tween people in the country. The black guy was dirty, by the way – like, really dirty – but that is beside the point.

Back to our home jungle. The park's order was not fol-lowed – one lion was killed after it killed three cows that belonged to Magezi Nsokoti, our fellow villager. The story made headlines in the news: Munghana Lonene FM broad-cast from the village, and Mlungisi Shivamba, the host of current affairs programme *Tiko Axi Etleli*, broadcast his show from Nkandziyi Primary School to look more deeply into the issue.

Bevhula still has its problems to this day: the Kruger National Park wants a buffer zone in the area, an issue that has divided the village in half. One group doesn't want the buffer zone. Then, there is Team Buffer Zone. In February 2018, those who were opposed to the chief's decision to allow the Kruger National Park the buffer zone were arrested. In retaliation, other villagers went to attack the chief's mansion by vandalising and setting fire to his house while he was inside. He had to be rescued by the police.

To be honest, I don't think Bevhula was supposed to be a human settlement. It was a very dangerous place for people to live in.

When my mom had finished collecting firewood, she would take a bucket and go to get water at a borehole, called *agwejeni*. It was further to the west of the village, towards Block H ka-Makahlule, next to Chief Bevhula's mansion. I was always fascinated by how she could walk upright with the bucket on her head, never using her hands to balance the bucket. To me, my mother was a magician. To this day, after studying the laws of physics, I don't understand how people are able to do that.

By this time, my father had found a job as a petrol attendant at the Shell garage in Thohoyandou. He was staying with my aunt, Mphephu Chauke – who was married to a Muvenda mechanic, George Nengovhela – in Itshani village, just outside Thohoyandou. My father would only come and visit us at month-ends.

Chapter 5

The mysterious fire

When we lived in Bevhula, we never visited anywhere. The furthest place I knew while staying at Bevhula was in town, ka-Malamulele. The one person who would visit town was my mom.

I remember visiting Malamulele only once. We woke up very early with my mother, because the taxis were very scarce. There was one taxi that went to town at 5:30 a.m. If you missed it, you could forget about your journey to town – or you would have to go hike at the intersection of the roads coming from Block C and Block H, which we called *a Kroseni*.

My mom made sure we got that taxi. The gravel road through the sandveld and mopane woodlands made the ride to Malamulele very uncomfortable. The taxi was overloaded. We sat next to the taxi conductor, who clearly didn't bath – his bad breath added to the awkwardness of the ride. He spoke to the driver all the way. When he opened his mouth, I simply couldn't take it. And when we joined the tarred road from ka-Mhinga, the potholes were worse than the gravel road.

We finally arrived. I marvelled at the town, with the shops and all. For the first time, my mother bought us clothes from Jet Stores. I was very glad and couldn't wait to go and brag to Sergeant. My mother always bought our clothes from the ladies who would come and sell clothes during the social grants payments. We called it *Amdendeni*. During this event, you would see little children who were supposed to be at school queuing in long lines to get money. *Amdendeni* was the biggest event in Bevhula. Hawkers from all over Malamulele would gather at Nkandziyi selling clothes, merchandise and goods for everyday use. We would bath and go there to see their displays. *Amdendeni* was more like the Durban July, but with no horses. Although, to be fair, one celebrity from the Durban July could easily buy out the whole *Amdendeni* event with little effort.

Poverty was rife in the village, so my mother decided to move back to our one-room shack in Atteridgeville to try to make ends meet.

Back in Limpopo, my mother hired Katekani Maswanganyi to be our guardian. She was well-mannered, and one of the few light-skinned ladies we had in the village. She looked after us. She was way older than us. She was in Grade 11 at Ntlhaveni High School in the neighbouring village, Block C ka-Makhuvele, which was about five kilometres from our village. There were a lot of bushes between the villages.

I remember Katekani failed to go to school the first day she moved into our home due to heavy rains. Bevhula, a low-lying area, was always at risk of flooding. We did not have a high school in our village. We didn't have a clinic or police station or shopping centre either.

The only thing we prided ourselves on having was a primary school and a tavern. Hollywood Tavern was its name, a reference to Hollywood in the States. It is where you would meet all the A-listers and who's-who of the village. We were very proud of our tavern, and it was always packed. In a place far away from industrial and commercial centres, a tavern is a nightclub and a grocery store all in one. Popular Xitsonga artist Matshwa Bemuda used to hang around Hollywood, since he stayed in the neighbouring village, ka-Nkovani.

Hollywood Tavern was my favourite spot in the village. I would normally hang around the tavern with my friend Sergeant. We would go there not to drink, but to watch the people who came to buy things there. Hollywood sold almost everything, from liquor to bread. The only competition that Hollywood had was a little shop that was far down the village next to Nkandziyi Primary School. The name of the shop was Mcbull, named after its owner. Mcbull looked like he came from Somalia or one of those regions. He dressed in Islamic clothing, wearing a thobe and a long beard. He also made a lot of money from the villagers.

While chilling with Sergeant at the entrance to Hollywood, I enjoyed watching some ladies who were always gambling. There was a game played called Mchayina, translated as 'the Chinese'. Mchayina was mostly played by middle-aged, ill-disciplined women, called *vabvana*. Most of them had children out of wedlock. These were the same people who would gamble using playing cards in Anyusitandi Ya Le Masirheni section. The decent

49

women of Bevhula didn't play Mchayina. By decent, I mean those who went to church or were married. If you played Mchayina, you were not a 'real woman'; if you were a man playing Mchayina, people would say you were bewitched.

Mchayina was an unauthorised lottery game. The dealer was a Chinese man, hence the name, who travelled around the Ntlhaveni villages in his 4 × 4 Toyota bakkie. He would select one winning number between 1 and 36. The villagers who played the game associated each number with a dream. If you had dreamt about drowning in water, you would play 3. If you dreamt about drinking water, you would play 13. If you dreamt about a female corpse, 14. If you dreamt about a criminal, 7. There was a checklist designed specifically for Mchayina. The regular players owned round wallets, also designed for Mchayina. If you had a good dream, you would go to one of those regular players. You would explain your dream and they would suggest a number associated with that number. If you were lucky enough to win, you would give her a share for using her wallet.

The Chinese man would come to Hollywood in the morning and was not allowed to repeat the same number when he came back later in the day. When he arrived at the tavern, no one would really see his face, because his bakkie had tinted windows. The only person who would see him was a woman who was in charge of collecting all the players' wallets and placing them into a huge bag. They would do an exchange: she would give him the bag, and he would immediately give her a small piece of paper with the winning number written on it. They would then usually wait a couple of minutes while he prepared the winning wallets. If you played a winning number with 50c, he would give you R14; for R1, R28; and for R1.50, R42. The higher the play value, the higher the return value, provided you won.

There were many rules associated with a winning number. For instance, if the winning number at ka-Mashobye, which was a neighbouring village, was 3, then the Chinese man wasn't allowed to use that number in our village. I remember that, one day, he betrayed the players. He used the same number he had used in the morning at Block C, a nearby village. This made the players in our village furious.

I heard one saying, '*Namuntlha xi koki mani?* (What is today's winning number?)'

Another responded, '*Nwana mhanee, veri xi koki fayifi a Block C, ivi xi tlhela xi koka yona na hala ka hina, xa hi tolovela* (My sister, he pulled number 5, the same number he pulled in Block C. He is messing with us).'

Sometimes, he would pull a number that had no winners. Sometimes, players would win in huge numbers, to the point where he would be unable to pay them. But they always had his back – they knew he would pay them the following day.

One day, when I was sitting with Sergeant in our usual spot on the huge cornerstone at the entrance of the tavern, I saw the Chinese man. I was very happy, but it was a very bad day for him. A police van had followed him to the tavern. When the woman handed him the big bag, the police took him out of his car and issued a warrant of arrest.

I heard one policeman say, '*Vanhu lava va dya mali ya midende ya vana hi mhaka wena* (These people are wasting their child support grants because of you).'

They drove away with him.

The Chinese man's arrest was the biggest crime scene I had ever seen in Bevhula. I didn't really care about the fact that he was in trouble – I just marvelled at how beautiful he was. In Bevhula, there were few light-skinned people. In fact, when I think about it now, almost everyone in Bevhula was very dark in complexion. The climate was characterised by very hot temperatures and people always laboured in the sun. So, almost everyone was very dark. In the village, we judged the beauty of a person by his or her skin tone. If people were light, they were beautiful; if they were dark, they were ugly. By this logic, almost everyone in Bevhula was ugly.

I was glad that I had seen the most beautiful man I had ever seen in my life.

The picture of the Chinese man stayed with me. I even went home to brag to Akani about what I had seen at the tavern.

By this time, I was a little bit older, so I could help my sisters out with household chores. They were learning to cook by this time. I remember Akani's food being terrible, and I would always complain: '*Sesi Akani mi sweki mbodza* (Sister Akani, your food is bad).' Akani never bought into my nonsense. She was very stubborn as a child and would push back: '*Voetsek, awu na nsati la* (Piss off, I'm not your wife)!'

And since I was the only boy in my household, I was obliged to fetch water from the borehole, which was very far away. I would push the wheelbarrow, in the ever-burning sun of Limpopo, and turn the handle to pump the water. I would get so hungry I would feel dizzy sometimes. And, on top of that, when I got home, the water would be salty. We also drew water from a well, which we drank because it was better than the salty water from the borehole.

During the summer, we would often have extremely hot, sunny days. I would pour water into the container we used for bathing and leave it in the sun. When it was time to bath, the water would be as warm as I liked it to be. That way, I could avoid going into the kitchen, which was terribly hot.

Each and every day, we endured the struggle of life in the village. With our parents five hundred kilometres away, life was not easy. Things reached a climax when our rondavel house was burned to ashes. Normally, we would sit around the fire in the kitchen until it was time for us to go to sleep. Despite our economic hardships, we lived lives filled with humour, warmth and love. There was no TV or radio. We would sing songs and play games. Katekani was our storyteller. We called her Garingani (Narrator). She would begin her storytelling by saying '*Garingani, N'wa-Garingani!* (I am Narrator, daughter of Narrator!)' after which we would cheer, 'Garingani!' We would cheer her name after each line of the story, until the story's end. We would tease one another, all four of us, my two sisters and our guardian. In winter, we bonded by playing while consuming the huge stockpile of firewood that my mother had left when she had gone to Pretoria.

Shortly after my mother left for Pretoria came the night-mare night in 2003, my earliest vivid memory. I will never forget that night. We had gone to sleep very early. I remember waking to huge confusion, filled with smoke and fire. I am the one who first noticed that the house that we were sleeping in was, in fact, on fire. I started screaming and shouting, waking my sisters and our guardian, Katekani. I shouted for help from our neigh-bour: '*Hahani Mavis! Hahani Mavis! Yindlu yatshwa! Ha fa!* (Aunt Mavis! Aunt Mavis! The house is burning! We are dying!)'

We were colliding with each other trying to escape. When Katekani reached for the door, for a moment we thought it had been locked from the outside. Luckily, it had just jammed, so we pushed it open and escaped. Our house was burning down before us. By the time the neighbours arrived, the thatched roof had crashed in, showering sparks. I remember us being outside in the deep of night in our underwear, crying at the tops of our voices. The neighbours stood around, watching the roof timbers and thatch, which my parents had collected by hand over many months, burn to the ground in an instant. Everything burned inside that rondavel. We were devastated.

The whole village was shocked by the tragedy, but everyone was happy that no life had been lost and no one had been hurt. What the villagers did not know was how hurt we were mentally. They did not know that we would bear the scar for a lifetime; the tragedy would haunt us for years to come.

For anyone who has never lived in a village, one thing I can tell you is that news travels faster than the speed of light. From Anyusitandi Ya Le Danwini to Anyusitandi Ya Le Masirheni, everybody knew about the fire. By the next morning, my mother already knew what had transpired at her house. She was devastated.

There she was, among the shacks, trying to provide for her children and, in an instant, as far as she knew, all her children were dead. I assume the thought of committing suicide came to her.

Later that day, someone more mature explained to her that no one had died but the house had burned down. She breathed a sigh of relief. My uncle, who stayed in the township where I was born, transported both my parents back home.

We did get support from family and friends from near and far. People of goodwill donated blankets and clothes to cover the damage. This was real communism, not the individualism, celebrated in the urban areas, that eventually leads to the capitalist approach in government. Life had to go on. The cause of the tragedy, who started the fire, remains a mystery to this day. It was a time of despair for all of us. We didn't know how to go on.

But the struggle had to go on. I remember walking to school barefoot for almost three weeks. The sun did not help: the ground was very hot, and I had to endure the pain. But most children walked barefoot to school. I was now one of them.

A few weeks later, my parents had to go back to Pretoria. I felt a little bit bitter about their leaving us behind in the midst of a trauma. We began to go downhill psychologically. After the fire, I remember social workers starting to come to our house. We would come home from school sometimes to find them talking to our guardian. They would look at us, and everything around us, as if we were orphans. They would ask a lot of questions. They worked with us to deal with the trauma that we were going through.

Some of the small-minded neighbours criticised my mother for moving to the city. Their argument was that it was milk and honey for my mother, while we were drowning in poverty. I heard one of the neighbours say, '*Va nga famba va ya joni va siya vana mara?* (How could she go to Gauteng and leave her children?)'

We had now moved into the rondavel kitchen. The once-upon-a-very-short-time bedroom had now become a kitchen without a roof, for it had burned down. We were, indeed, drowning in poverty.

Our family was so poor that we ate *majakiti*, which was basically fried grass, and *guxe* or *thelele* which, on the surface, looked like mucus. Don't get me wrong, this type of food was, and still is, nice, but the problem is that we ate it repeatedly – to a point at which we lost our appetite. During that time, we would also go into the wild to find locusts, mopane worms, crickets and other insects as an alternative food source. But, since it was common food in the village, it almost felt normal. I learnt that, when you suffer together, no one can really laugh at you, so you end up feeling good. It was a close community. Almost everyone knew everyone.

Due to the horrible food we ate, and Akani's cooking skills, I would often visit my step-grandmother in the old stead. I would go there at dinnertime. I knew that she knew exactly why I was there; she never embarrassed me by asking, since visiting was part of showing our deep affection for each other. She would dish up for me. She was the kind of cook who would fill your plate with food such as pap, chicken feet, beetroot and cabbage. I would eat like there was no tomorrow. The more I ate, the better she felt. House visiting was a wonderful feature of our way of life in the village. My grandmother would say, '*Dyana nwana nwananga uta kula* (Eat so you can grow, my grandson).' We got along because she was very talkative, just like I was. Chicken feet and heads, and tinned pilchards, were really a luxury for me.

She would sometimes give me money. I would go and buy *ti baki* fish (baked fish) at Hollywood Tavern. *Baki* fish was the best treat in the whole village. The elites of the village ate it.

After our home was destroyed, the challenges persisted. In the kitchen that we slept in, we would kill snakes week in and week out, to a point where we were afraid to go to sleep at night. During the day, everything was fine; the problem was at night when it was time to sleep.

It was not long until my mother took us back to Pretoria.

Chapter 6

Return to Pretoria

After hearing our concerns, my mother decided to take us back to our one-room shack in Atteridgeville. '*Swa antswa loko ni hlupheka na nwina kwala mkhukhwini than loko mi ri kule na mina* (It is better if we struggle together in this shack than you being far away from me),' said my mother.

Curtains divided our one-room shack into the section where my parents slept and the section where my two sisters and I slept. During the day, our bedroom was the kitchen. For us, it was not a big deal. We were used to sleeping in the kitchen.

Immediately after the Easter holidays, in April 2004, my mother enrolled us at Masizane Primary School. It was situated in the centre of Selbourne Side, on the corner of Makuruntsi and Madisha streets, not far from the double-storey Edward Phatudi Comprehensive School in the east and another Vhavenda primary school to the west, called Thohoyandou. To the north was an Engen garage owned by Bushy Makwakwa; to the south was Mackaya Street, where we used to live when I was born.

The school had five blocks, with a toilet block facing Makuruntsi Street and the other four blocks on either side forming a C shape. The entrance was in Makuru-ntsi Street. The administration block was behind all the five blocks, at the Madisha Street entrance. Masizane was a no-fee school, but we paid in so many ways – from buying raffle tickets, to paying for a jumping castle, to being forced to pay to watch movies in the school hall, to paying the magician who would come and perform his tricks. We *really* paid school fees.

On my first day – wearing my navy-blue trousers and yellow shirt, and Tsakani and Akani wearing their black *dangaras* from Nkandziyi – I was very perplexed. The challenge for me was to mix with the other kids, who were speaking different languages. Tsakani and Akani had already found new friends, but I was still fascinated by everything. I had never drunk alcohol or smoked cig-arettes, and here I saw little children my age (ten years old) doing all those things. Those kids also used *tsotsi-taal* (slang) expressions that were just as new to me, such as *akere* and *exsay* and *exwaar* and *dintshang?* and *my bro*. Every night, as I lay on the floor, I would flash back to these words.

In Pretoria, the most common languages were Setswa-na, isiZulu and *tsotsitaal*. *Tsotsitaal* was a mixture of languages such as Afrikaans, Sesotho, English and isi-Zulu that kids used to form a unique township language. I did not understand these languages. The fact that I had been born there did not matter – it was a different world.

The Tswana kids always teased me. They made fun of how I spoke. I could not even understand their language, so I had to have a translator when I communicated with them. They called me 'Buti' (brother) and 'Hosi' (chief). Even though I found it a bit offensive at times, they really thought they were respecting me. There was one kid I liked. His name was Peter Nkwe. He would always say, '*Exsay, brayaka* (Hey, my brother),' then proceed to whatever he wanted to say. Peter was very light-skinned, and always teased me. He would come to me and say, '*Exsay, brayaka Blacky* (Hey, my brother Blacky),' and the other kids would laugh. Everyone treated Peter well. I guess it's because of his complexion. Light-skinned kids were always favoured, even if they were douchebags like him. The other Tswana kids teased me as much as Peter did.

I later realised that we Vatsonga were not really considered people in society. The other kids at school were really feeding off their parents. With the stigma that came with being a Mutsonga, other Vatsonga learners were even afraid to speak Xitsonga among themselves. This is a common trend for Vatsonga, especially in urban areas – they are more likely to switch to dominant languages in order to fit in. We have an identity crisis – which comes, of course, comes from centuries of racial, tribal and religious oppression! I spoke very deep Xitsonga loudly. I didn't really have feelings about being a Shangaan, as they called us, because I was trying so hard, in every way I could, to be Tswana or Pedi. So I ended up learning other languages and became integrated with the Tswanas and Pedis and Zulus – but you would always tell that I was Shangaan, for I was very dark, loud, and always shining on the face.

I would eat from the feeding scheme during lunch breaks, as money for lunches was very little – assuming there was any at all. The menu consisted of brown bread with margarine, peanut butter and jam, served with a powdered milkshake supplement. This was better than the food we ate at Nkandziyi.

I was a heavy eater, which did not help me since we were poor. After school – on my way back home, which was five hundred metres away – Brayaka Peter (my brother Peter) would show me around. Sometimes, instead of going home after school, I would walk to the taxi rank with him, and hang around where things like apples and sweets were displayed in plastic bags and baskets. I would wait for my chance to steal a banana or some chips. I remember I once got caught. The man from whom I stole threatened to come to my home. I was very anxious that night, and could not sleep. Little did I know that he did not even know where I lived: our squatter camp was a very messy and complicated place, and had a lot of alleys in which stinking water would run. My little mind failed to comprehend that; I quit stealing that day. If my mother had found out, I swear, she would have beaten me to death.

When I stopped stealing, I also stopped hanging out with Brayaka Peter. I had met some other Vatsonga whose parents were from Limpopo. Brian Baloyi, who lived not far from the school in Keena Street, was from Oliphantshoek (a Holofani) village. Success Nobela was from ka-Mavabe village. Success didn't stay very far from our home. This meant that we hung around together, at school and after school. Success went on to become my best friend up to matric. We were in the same class from Grade 4 to Grade 12.

Katlego Ngobeni was the youngest among us. He had skipped a grade because he was smart. He was born in 1996. He stayed in Atteridgeville's Extension 7. He is the one who would always pick up girls – he had the charm, while Success and I were really shy. Later, in 2005, came a little girl from Limpopo. Her name was Nyeleti Maluleke. Our class teacher, Diner Sebola, assigned her to sit with me. Nyeleti was my darling. Since we were desk mates, Nyeleti was my girlfriend. She didn't know this, because I never proposed to her, but let us not focus on that for now. David Mathe was the eldest in our class. He was born in 1991. He came to school when he wanted to, or when he was bored at home with whatever he was doing: it was quite clear that he had other commitments. In fact, David was a part-time learner. Between him and Katlego, there was a five-year age difference.

I enjoyed mathematics class. Milton Ngobeni was our maths teacher. Mr Ngobeni was very funny, and he made our class fun. He would stand in front of our class, which had a huge chalkboard, and divide the class according to how we had scored in our tests. He would give each group the name of a school around Pretoria. We had Sunrise, which was a school for average students. Zodwa was a special school. Weskoppies was a school for mentally ill learners. And Masizane was our school. Our class had four rows. The first row was called Masizane; the A students sat there. The second row was Sunrise, where the B students sat. The third row was Zodwa, where the C students sat. And the last one was Weskoppies. That's where the struggling students sat. Nyeleti Themba, Pfukani Shingange, George Mathe and Katlego Ngobeni were the kings of Masizane. Dorothy Nukeri, Sophy Make and Leleti Nxumalo were the queens of Weskoppies. I was moving around Sunrise and Masizane. I sat in Weskoppies only once.

Mr Mabasa was my favourite teacher. He used to call me *n'wana boti* (my brother's son), the reason being that Mabasa and Chauke were of the same clan. Mr Mabasa knew me from the athletics team before teaching me Xitsonga in Grade 7. I used to come first in athletics at school, but when we went out to white schools like Laerskool Rooihuiskraal in Centurion, the white kids would outrun me. Mr Mabasa was my cheerleader. He would often say, '*N'wana boti, a va nge ku siyi wena valungu lava* (My son, you shall outrun these whites).'

By the time I got to Grade 7 in 2007, I was elected as a class prefect. I was also in the scholar patrol, where we used to help other kids cross the road in the morning to get to school. We patrolled Hlakola Street, next to the Engen garage, every morning.

I had become a real fan of wrestling. Since we did not have the luxury of owning a television, I was always at my friend Mbuyelo Mugwedi's home. I enjoyed the way the wrestlers confronted each other. I was a big fan of The Rock, Dwayne Johnson. He was very mischievous. I also loved John Cena, with his gimmicks and swag.

One thing I liked about wrestling was that, after a

major event, new feuds began. Years later, I came to realise that this is how life really is. When we were still in preschool, we could not wait to go to elementary school. There, we fantasised about getting to Grade 7. There, we longed to graduate and go to high school. There, we wanted to see ourselves in matric. Having got there, we were so eager to go to university. There, we were dying to go to the world of work – only to work tirelessly for promotions. The cycle went on and on, it was for a similar reason that Nelson Mandela observed that, 'after climbing a great hill, one only finds that there are many more hills to climb'.

We are born with a weakness called discontent; I see each stage in life as a new fight to be fought.

I enjoyed watching television at my friend's house. I liked how they would chase me away at dinnertime by saying that my mother was calling me. I would get home to discover that she hadn't called me. It happened every time, without fail.

Seeing me struggling, my mother soon bought us a TV. But our TV was not as big as Mbuyelo's TV. It had no remote control. Even the visuals were not the same – it was a black-and-white TV. The worst part for me is that the TV played the SABC channels only, and e.tv aired wrestling. I never appreciated that TV. I never appreciated my mother's efforts in buying something for us.

But my sisters were happy with our TV: they were no fans of wrestling. They watched the popular soapies *Generations* and *Muvhango. Generations* usually showed black people of the Tswana, Xhosa and Zulu tribes rising to powerful positions and owning big companies. It rarely showed a township or a village. *Muvhango* was similar to *Generations*, but showed a civilised Vhavenda tribe. *Muvhango* was screened twice a week on Mondays and Tuesdays; *Generations* played on weekdays. These soapies played a huge role in my life, presenting an ideal that my sisters and I wanted to live up to.

But today, I watch them with great contempt. They are not a true representation of black life. What soapies such as *Generations* and *Muvhango* show is that black people are living the good life, which is not true. In the same way as people call the children born in 1994 born-frees, it is false!

After school, we would watch *Takalani Sesame* with Akani. Her favourite character was Neno, and mine was Moshe. After watching *Takalani*, I would have to go and get water from the JoJo tank. I would take the wheelbarrow and wait for my crush, Nomthandazo Gatsheni, at the gate. She lived in our street. When she saw me, she would fetch her wheelbarrow and we would go together. After collecting the water, I would go to Success's place, or to Mbuyelo's place to watch *Dragon Ball Z* cartoons.

At night, we would watch the soapies. Since we changed channels manually on the TV, the switch broke, and we had to use pliers. This was great for me, because I was the only one who knew how to change the channels: I knew how many turns were needed to get to SABC 1 and how many to SABC 2. I called all the shots. When we clashed on Mondays – Akani would want to watch *Muvhango*, while I would want to watch *MTN Soccer*

Zone – I would simply take the pliers and put them away. My mother would intervene. She would always favour Akani: '*N'wi cinceli a vona xitori kwalano* (Help her change the channel).' So, my father would defend me: '*Hay, tshi-ka mfana a vona bolo. Yi tlanga kanwe phela, mfana wa mina anga languti TV* (No, leave my boy. He only watches this once).'

Tsakani would sit there quietly as all four of us debated.

Akani was very stubborn. I lost most fights with her, even physical ones: she used to beat me very badly. It was out of Akani's stubbornness that I started watching *Generations*, and I was hooked. My favourite character was Khaphela Ngcobo, played by Mike Mvelase. I liked his rural appeal in civilised Johannesburg. Everything about his character was funny – his beard and outfit, and how he never adapted to Johannesburg. I would make as if I was teasing Khaphela whenever he appeared, and the whole family would laugh.

Humour played a huge role in our family, despite our economic struggles. We got it from our parents. We would usually assign funny names to our neighbours and the people who came to visit our home. These, of course, were inside jokes. We called the lady who sold chicken feet on our street corner N'wa-Thakeni (The Dirty One). We called our neighbour Nhloko (Head) because of his big head. The Mozambican man who used to fix our shoes we called Shorty. Shorty was a dwarf. (His real name was Philmon Chauke. All the Mozambican immigrants I knew called themselves Chauke, it being one of the most popular surnames in our tribe.) My father called a lady who sold goods at the nearest tavern Basuluka (Dry Skin). During their girl talks, my mom and sisters called my father Nghomunghomu, after a neighbouring village back at Bevhula. When they saw my father coming, they would say, '*Nghomu hi valavo* (Here comes Nghomu). They called me Bunjai, after a crazy man, July Njhembheza, who grew up with my mother. They shortened Buti July to Bunjai. July Njhembheza was a psychopath, and they believed I was like him in many ways. They would sing a short song that Akani had composed. It went '*July Njhembheza u tshama ntsungeni, ntsungeni lowuya . . . ntsungeni wa Ritavi'* (July Njhembheza stays on the far shore of the Letaba River).' When I was young, I used to cry when they sang the song, for it was a very emotional song. Still, judging by the records and statistics, it's safe to say that Akani was a savage.

By this time, I had started to make a small garden for spinach in the yard outside our shack. But water was scarce; the plants would just dry out. I felt a bit nostalgic. I missed Limpopo, for some strange reason. I really wanted to grow veggies: I had heard that this kind of food made you stronger as a man. I did not want to grow weak from living the city life.

I was too serious for my age . . .

Chapter 7

Clinton, you are not a man

In 2006, it was time for me to go for circumcision. My mother didn't want me to go to the initiation school. Her religious beliefs didn't allow her to take me to the mountain. If she took me to the mountain, she would have been suspended from her church for a period of seven years. She never wanted to take that chance!

There was a bit of tension between my parents – my father was not a religious person, although he used to practise a bit of African religion. Time and again, he would communicate with the spirit elders or ancestors. Before he embarked on a trip or a new job or any major event, he would pour snuff. It didn't matter where, though. He would pour snuff on the ground while reciting his wishes. He never went to church. He was against the ideas of pastors, and very critical of them. When he had problems, he would often say, '*He vafana, va le hansi ava tsakangi kam, swilava munhu aya kaya a ya phahla* (Hey buddy, the ancestors are unhappy, maybe it's time I go down to the village for rituals).'

I remember he once took me. We arrived in Axikhulu, at my step-grandmother's house, since our home had been destroyed. In the morning, we woke up very early and went to the back yard, where the tombstone of my grandmother was located. We started off by removing the small weeds around it. Then my father poured a cupful of *umqombothi* that my stepgrandmother had prepared as an offering.

He took out some snuff and gave it to me. '*Vulavula na kokwani wa wena* (Speak to your grandmother).'

I took it and recited my wishes while I was putting snuff at the head of the tombstone: '*Kokwani, hi mina Clinton ntukulu wa nwina, mi hi pfumelela tindlela kokwani* (Granny, it's your grandson Clinton. Please bless us).'

My father said, '*Mhani, mi dzahisana na vo papa kweleno* (Mom, please share the snuff with Dad over there),' which made me very curious.

'*Mara papa, va ta dzahisana njhani?* (But Dad, how are they going to share snuff?)'

My father responded, '*Vanhu lava waswinwe sweswi* (They are together now).'

Because of my father's proud African heritage, he wanted me to go to the initiation school. It was believed that if a male doesn't go to the mountain, he is not a man. '*Wanuna wa mampela uya entshaveni mfana mina* (A real man goes to initiation school, my boy).'

In the end, my mother's argument won, just like in any argument between a man and a woman. We know who wins these things; there was nothing surprising there. So, I ended up being circumcised at a surgery. My mother sent me to Shirley village, where I would join my cousins Oscar and Nhlamulo.

Before I left Gauteng during the school holidays in June for Elim, my father, who had changed his mind about initiation school, became supportive. He told me that the process was very easy. That all that would happen is that I would get there and take my clothes off, then lie in bed. The doctor would just put a big machine on top of my penis, then my foreskin would be gone. I believed him. I was only twelve years old.

I was very happy about the process as explained by my father: my friend Mbuyelo, who had gone through a traditional circumcision, had told me how painful it had been. Mbuyelo proclaimed that he would rather have died than gone to a hospital, because going to a hospital doesn't make you a man.

Mbuyelo was Team Mountain, and more than willing to share his experiences. He told me that it involved boys camping for weeks, secluded from their families and women, learning lessons from their elders. A few years later, I noted as the initiates came back from the mountain in Atteridgeville that what Mbuyelo had said was the case. When the initiates came back from Thobejani (the man who was responsible for the school), the celebrations were enormous. There was a great deal of alcohol consumed by those in attendance, their parents ululating and shouting.

When I asked the *swigamatshuku* (initiates) why they'd had to go through all this, they replied, '*Go thatha go ba mmuna, a go rekiwi* (It's hard to be a man. You can't buy it, but you have to experience it).'

And when I asked further about the importance of what

they had done, they continued, '*O ntswantse oe thuthe go gothlelela gore he mathatha a bophelo a fithla, o tlo kgona go a fenya* (You have to endure the hardships so that, when times get tough in your life, you know how to get through them).'

The *swigamatshuku* sang beautiful songs about their ordeal. Their seclusion and suffering represented the trials of life; the experience was a test of personal character.

Mbuyelo said they removed their foreskins very brutally using a sharp knife, and then the initiates surrendered their names. They were smeared with a brownish paste to mark the final stage of the transition to manhood. I know he was right, because my father also surrendered his name. His other name, Hlengani, he got at the initiation school.

So, when my father told me that a surgery circumcision was pain-free, I was very happy. Until I got to the doctor in Waterval township, a few metres from Shirley village, with my two cousins. As we waited in the reception of a big house that sat on a small hill, I heard a boy screaming his lungs out in the procedure room. At first I thought I was hearing things, but as the second boy went in, I realised that my friend who had gone to the traditional school may have been right after all. It was not long until I was called in. The first thing I saw was the foreskins in the dustbin. I could feel the pain merely by looking at those foreskins. When I saw the hospital bed in the centre of the room, I realised my fate was inevitable.

The doctor told me to take off my trousers. I was very

uncomfortable because there were two guys in the room and one lady. She made me very uncomfortable. I sat on top of the bed. The doctor was very friendly. He talked me into it; within seconds, I was naked.

'*Unge twi nchumu mfo*' (You won't feel any pain, bro).'

He took my little penis and brushed it, looking for a vein. He then injected my penis, and I screamed louder than the little boy before me had. The pain was simply unbearable. I'd heard that birth pains were strong, but I don't think anything could compare with the pain I felt that day. By the second injection, I wanted to leave, but the two buff guys in the room grabbed me. By the time the doctor cut my foreskin with a pair of scissors, I didn't feel even a little pain. I watched him stitch me the same way my mom used to sew my trousers. Then he bandaged me.

'*Mi to yima ma vhiki ma 4 Cawuke, then mita va right* (Just wait for four weeks, Mr Chauke, then you will be all right).'

I then left the room with my prescription. I went back to the reception and waited for my two cousins to get their pains. Walking home later, I was very angry with my father for misleading me. I blamed him for all the pain I was feeling. I couldn't even walk properly.

While my uncle Godfrey was taking care of us, I believed that I would never, ever recover. The recovery period felt like a year. But, just like the doctor had said, after four weeks, I had recovered. When I went back to Gauteng, even though I had undergone the painful process of having my foreskin removed, my father still thought I was not man enough. He called me Leshuburi and the Xhosa guys called me Inkwenkwe. These names were harsh insults, because they meant a boy who has not yet graduated to manhood.

Retrospectively, though, I don't wish I had gone to the mountain instead, because I don't agree with their description of what a 'real man' was.

Chapter 8

The sacrifices of my mother

My mother and I fought a lot when I was still very young. I thought she was very hard on me. But, later, I came to realise that she was playing two roles in my life: of both mother and father.

My first realisation of this was when I saw my mother working as a bricklayer constructing RDP houses in the neighbouring township of Lotus Gardens. The RDP houses were sold, and not awarded to deserving poor people. My uncle Godfrey, who had come from Limpopo in 2004, bought a house in Lotus Gardens Phase 2. This didn't sit well with my mother: she had applied for an RDP house in 1998, and followed up through the years, but she never got anything. Had the government officials not been corrupt, they could have been more influential here.

It was a very painful thing to see my twenty-four-year-old uncle getting a house in the blink of an eye when people like Kokwane Va Le Bush, who was seventy-five years old, had waited for an RDP house all their lives. The councillors' and politicians' corruption was just brutal. The sad part of the RDP story is that my mother constructed those same houses. Every time she complained about her back pain, she always pointed back to that project. Soon after the project ended, the workers were retrenched and my mom became unemployed.

The only things that got us through that period were the social grants we received from the government. The social grants were administered by the South African Social Security Agency (SASSA) to ensure the provision of comprehensive social security services against the vulnerability and poverty faced by families like ours. The child support grant was given to eligible children who were up to fifteen years old. By 2008, Akani and Tsakani were no longer getting social grants because they were older than fifteen. I was the only one receiving money from the government, and it carried our family.

After an electioneering visit by ANC presidential nominee Jacob Zuma at the Atteridgeville community hall in March 2008, Zuma promised to increase the age of eligibility of the recipients from fifteen to eighteen. This was great news for my mother. From that moment, my mother hoped that Zuma would get elected on those grounds: '*A va nwi hlawuli, kumbe swilo aswi ta hi olovela* (Let them elect him, perhaps things will be easier for us).'

Jacob Zuma was a very controversial political figure who had over seven hundred criminal charges against him. But, since he promised us the grants, my mother didn't care. After his election to the presidency, Zuma kept his promise and our family's standard of living improved. At that stage, I had ambivalent feelings about him. This was a topic that I always discussed with my elders. Both my parents supported Zuma all the way, and still do to this day. I had to battle very hard to resolve the contradictions that Zuma presented in my life.

Despite our economic struggles, we lived a joyful life. My father was the one who frequently spoiled our fun. The main reason for this was his consumption of alcohol. Alcohol made him lose his faculties. He would swear a lot in front of us, and I would subconsciously lose more respect for him. He didn't really understand that he was still in the process of raising us. He drank *umqombothi* and *mbhambha*. *Mbhambha* was brewed in a similar way to how my step-grandmother brewed *umqombothi*, but it was weaker.

My father would frequently come home drunk, with his stuff in a two-litre bottle, being held up by a person on either side of him because our home was on a small hill. He would start to fight with my mother. In fact, he would fight with all of us.

After their confrontations, my mother would simply look at me and say, '*Nwanaga, unga nwi byala unga ta fana na papa wena* (Don't ever drink alcohol, because you will end up like your father).'

It's advice I never forget, wherever I go.

My father was a very quiet man when he was sober. If he had an issue, he wouldn't solve it until he came home late at night, drunk. In the morning, he would often ask what had happened the previous night: '*Kasi why mini kwateleni?* (Why are angry with me?)'

I would reply, '*Ani nwina ami dakwini tolo* (Because you were drunk yesterday).'

My mother would intervene and say, '*Munhu lonkulu*

76

anga vuriwi ku dakwa. Veri ami xurhimi (You can't say your father was drunk. Rather say he was a bit tipsy).'

What I was learning at school was very different from what I was learning at home. I only realised later that I was getting a true education at home. At school, I always felt like I was being brainwashed, but at home my mother seemed to provide a better alternative. She encouraged independent thinking and taught good morals to live by.

Kokwane Va Le Bush would usually take my mother to work in Laudium, a neighbouring suburb where rich Indians lived. I would overhear Kokwane Va Le Bush say, '*Unga landzeleli nuna wa wena loko anga lavi ku tirha, wena famba tirhela vana va wena* (Don't mind your husband, just focus on providing for your children).'

My mother would go to clean and iron on Mondays and Wednesday. On Tuesdays, Thursdays and Fridays, she would babysit a child in Lotus Gardens on the Indian side of the township. And on weekends, she would wash the clothes of the man who would insult her while she was providing for him.

It was too much for her and she ended up saying, '*Clili, u fanele ku dyondza ku ti hlantswela* (Clili, you must learn to wash your own clothes).' I started washing my own clothes when I was thirteen years old. When I went to play in our dusty street, I would be a little careful because I knew the pain of washing.

At this age, I used to wet my bed. My mom would always be at my throat in the morning. '*Clinton! I nwana waka mani unwani u nwi vonaku a neka minkumba la*

77

mgangeni? (Clinton! Who else wets the blankets around here?)' she would ask while preparing a belt to whip me. When we bought something to drink late at night, they wouldn't give me any of it. This served as a punishment. I stopped wetting my bed because of it.

My mother once took me to her workplace. '*Ahi fambi la ni tirhaku kona ku loko no jela, uta ni landza* (Let's go to my workplace, so you can fetch me if I get stuck),' she said. I woke up very early in the morning and went down to the taxi rank in Maunde Street. When the Atteridgeville Bus Service (ABS) bus dropped us in Laudium, I was so thrilled by the beauty of the houses I saw around me. We walked a good hundred metres up a small, hilly street towards the house where my mother worked. When we got to the gate, my mom opened it using a remote control. The owner of the house seemed to trust my mom, because she had given her the keys. Her job was to clean; after that, she went back home.

The house had about five bedrooms, a dining room and a kitchen that was as big as our shack yard. It had two entrances, one in front and the other at the back, which led you to the beautiful garden. On the left of it was a big swimming pool and on the right was a cage with one big dog. Upon seeing the dog, I went back inside the house. I marvelled at Mrs Naidoo's house. I know her name because there were a lot of her certificates displayed on the walls between the dining room and the library. I walked around the house while my mother cleaned it and did all the household chores.

Mrs Naidoo was a single parent and had only one son,

who stayed at a boarding school. When my mother's shift was over and we went home, I was angry that my mother's employer's house was so big and beautiful. I couldn't comprehend how the five of us had to live in our shack while Mrs Naidoo lived alone in a very big house.

My mother taught me about hard work and the importance of education by dropping small and subtle hints that I had to aspire to be somebody important in life. She would often say, '*Nwananga mina ani dyondzangi xikolo, ni lava nwina mi dyondzeka* (I am uneducated and I want you to be educated).' She may never have gone far at school, but I came to have high regard for her intellect. She may not have spoken English properly, and she lacked academic jargon, but she was sharp as a whip. She couldn't read. When I was still very young, I used to lose my patience while reading stuff to her or storing numbers on her phone. I thought she was dumb for not being able to read. Despite that, she raised me and my two sisters; even though we were shack poor, as a little child I never felt that we were because she would cover it up well with wisdom and a tender heart.

One sad day in March 2009, she came home from work limping. '*Ni lumi hi mbyana vananga* (My children, I was bitten by a dog),' she said. She explained how she had been attacked by the dog at Mrs Naidoo's house. Had Mrs Naidoo not been at home, the dog may have killed her. This made me furious. I wanted to go to Mrs Naidoo's house and confront her for her evil negligence. I was very young and naïve. But my mom brushed it off and said, '*Ani hina ahi dyondzangi xikolo, hi tirha walowu wa makhixi, hi famba hi lumiwa na hi timbyana* (Since I am not educated, I struggle with domestic work to the point of being attacked by the dogs).'

She was admitted to Kalafong Hospital for two days.

After recovering from the dog bite, my mom decided to become self-employed again. She began selling spinach, the job she was doing when she had met my father in Eyethu in 1988. She joined some other ladies who used to collect spinach from a plot close to the Hartebeespoort Dam. They were transported by an old man named Shivambu. He would drop them there and collect them later, charging them for transport. Upon her return, she would put a basket of spinach on her head and embark on a lonely journey of selling it in the hilly streets of Atteridgeville and Saulsville.

She also used Shivambu's car to fetch dry grass on the mountain just above our shacks towards Laudium. In winter, she sourced wild grass from the forest. Back home, she would dry the grasses and patiently knit them into long pieces. She would then tie the pieces up to make a broom, using a piece of tyre tube which she would have asked me to prepare. She made beautiful brooms, which she sold in the same way as she sold spinach. The wild grass above our squatter camp helped her contribute to our family's income.

Looking back at my mother's life, I wonder if they will ever erect a stature in her honour. I am very sceptical about them ever renaming one of the streets in the city after her. I doubt she will ever make it into a *Greatest South Africans* book. I don't know if the kids at school

80

will ever learn about her. I have no hope that they will ever make 22 January a public holiday – her birthday, of course. In my life, I have never met anyone with greater integrity, perseverance, strength or intellect, or a better work ethic, than her. To this day, my mother remains a constant pillar of strength.

Chapter 9

The battle of religions

What kept my mother going through the storms of her life was her deep-rooted faith in God. She was a devoted member of the Zion Christian Church (ZCC), which took its name from Biblical references to Mount Zion. My mother attended the main church, pastored by Engenas Lekganyane, wearing a star badge. She always took us with her. The church was at the top of a steep hill in Thindisa Street, not far away from the Lucas Moripe Stadium. She always took us with her.

One street away was the Ten Morgan Cemetery in Maunde Street, the entrance to Atteridgeville from Laudium. Ten Morgan Cemetery is where my great-grandmother is buried. And since ZCC beliefs emphasised the healing power of religious faith despite occasional conflicts with traditional African religious beliefs, especially those concerning the power of the ancestors to intercede on behalf of humans, it respected those beliefs. It combined African traditional values with Christian faith. This always confused me: I would occasionally see my mom going to do her rituals in a similar way to how my father did his, by using snuff and cleaning her grandmother's tomb. She would often say, '*Swilava munhu aya hlakula a sirheni ra kokwane* (I shall go and clean my grandmother's tomb).' The only difference between my mom and my dad was that my mom felt it was unnecessary for us to go with her. '*Ahi maxaka ya ka nwina kokwani, wena u waka Chauke mina niwa ka Baloyi* (You are not related to my grandmother – I am from the Baloyi clan and you are from the Chauke clan),' she would say. So, ultimately, her grandmother would be unable to bless me, she explained. Nepotism in its highest form!

On Sundays, she would take us to church in Thindisa Street. She also had a funeral policy with the church. Sometimes, she would forgo the main service and go there only to pay for the policy and come back. And, on a Saturday, I would see my mother going to Ten Morgan. It always perplexed me that my mother's places of worship – which, on the surface, looked to be in contrast – were, in fact, very close, not only in proximity but also in practice.

When we left for church, my father would simply say, '*Fambani mi ya khongela vafundhisi va nwina* (Go and worship your pastors).' We were required to wear jerseys all the time and my sisters were supposed to cover their hair. If they did not, they wouldn't be allowed in.

At the gate, they sprinkled us with water on our faces. We turned our backs to them, and they sprinkled our backs. Finally, they poured some into our hands. We either drank it or washed our hands with it, and made our way in.

My mom wore a blue dress for church services. Since I was still young, it was not compulsory for me to wear the military-style khakis, police-style hat and star badge that the older guys wore.

In the service, there were two groups of people. One group was the ladies who danced a dance called *mmpogo*. The other group was the guys on the side, who would be dancing *mukhukhu*. Later, they would converge; both would sing *mmpogo* for a long time, and finally change to one or two songs. '*Ramarumo wa kolobejta, hi vona Papa Yeso*' ('Ramarumo blesses us as we see Jesus's father') was my favourite song. Ramarumo Lekganyane was believed to have supernatural powers and to be the mediator between man and God. This is the reason why most worship songs were about him. My mom would say, '*Nwinyi wa hina u na matimba* (Our Lord [Lekganyane] is powerful).'

After singing, we settled down for a short sermon, which would be mostly announcements about the church's upcoming events. Women were not allowed to take part in Sunday service preaching. They were allowed to preach during the women's services held every Wednesday. My mom used to attend those services. They also took money for offering.

The ZCC was about peace and respect and the love of God. The church preached the message of peace. When my mom met a person wearing a ZCC badge, she would say, '*Kgotsong* (Peace be unto you).' The response would be, '*Ayateng* (Let it be so).'

Since apartheid was a racially and religiously motivated ideology, the ZCC sought freedom using the Bible. The church sought to rewrite history, taking the game from the country's former masters. Lekganyane was our cult. He was believed to have supernatural powers and to be the mediator between man and God. When members got baptised, they would be baptised in the three names of the founders of the church – Barnabas, Edward and Engenas Lekganyane – instead of in the names of the Trinity!

As opposed to the mainstream European churches, the ZCC has sought independence in terms of its theological approach. Many people do not understand the ZCC's approach to Christianity. This is still the case with Bazalwane (members of the Pentecostal church). Having been thoroughly brainwashed by the European churches through the apartheid education system, in which Africans and their beliefs were rejected and mocked, they saw the ZCC as a faction. They used to laugh at us, and proclaimed that we were in the darkness.

During the Easter holidays, my mom would join millions of other ZCC members and make her pilgrimage to the church's headquarters at Zion City Moria in Limpopo province. There, they would meet Bishop Lekganyane and pray for blessings. Even if she didn't have money, she would make a plan not to pass up the chance of receiving blessings. Before she went to Moria, she would often first go to Ten Morgan to ask for a safe journey from her grandmother – the roads would be flooded with people going to Moria and other worship centres.

The church still believed in prophecy, the power of healing, and spiritual counselling. My mother had a strong belief in prophets and prophecies. They would prophesy during our services in Thindisa Street. The prophet or prophetess would simply come, looking rather devastated, and point at my mother. From there, she would follow their lead. They usually gave her a prescription called *taelo* that was also sold in the church, such as Vaseline, salt and coffee with a photo of Lekganyane. When she got *taelo*, she would call me. I would wear a jersey then mix it for her.

The different mechanisms for faith healing included the laying on of hands, the use of holy water, drinking blessed tea with no sugar (called *muhavulu*) and coffee, and wearing blessed cords or cloth. I remember my mother buying me a blessed cord, called *ntlamu*. I had to wear it around my waist. She would say, '*Loko wo chuncha ntlamu wolowo, uta fa* (If you untie that cord, you will probably die).' So, *ntlamu* was a literal chain – one of the chains I refer to in the title of this book.

My mom bought the church magazine, called *Messenger*. I enjoyed paging through the photos hoping to find her, and would be disappointed if I didn't. The magazine updated the members about the church's upcoming events, such as a visit from the bishop or where the church's brass band, called *diphala*, would be performing. She also bought a photo of Lekganyane and placed it in our kitchen. She would simply say, '*Nwinyi wa hina wa hi sirhelela* (Our Lord is watching over us).'

It seemed like my mother's prayers were working. By 2008, my father had improved his lazy tendencies. He worked as a mechanic, taxi driver, plumber and other blue-collar jobs in and around Gauteng. I did not think that my father was putting more effort in than my mother, though. But I did appreciate him because he was always part of our lives – unlike some of my friends' fathers, who were either altogether absent or did not come back home on a regular basis. In many African families, fathers were absent, so it was common for mothers to become both parents at the same time. Some fathers had run away and rejected parenthood of their children. Some were away for work. Some had been arrested. Some had passed away.

By 2009, my father was in his third year working for the contractor that manufactured cement at Iscor in Pretoria West. My mother told us it was the job our father had held for the longest – until one depressing day, when my father came home from work very early. Normally, he came home very late. He had been injured at work when about ten bags of cement had fallen onto him. My father was a very strong man. Because of his pride, he never showed weakness or pain in front of us. But, on that day, he was in great pain. He could hardly move his body, and his legs were paralysed. He was then taken to Kalafong Hospital and got help.

It always hit me, though: why had they not taken him to hospital from his workplace? But my father always played the hero, so I guess he had refused to go.

To this day, my father lives on disability grants. He lost his job and took his former employers to the Commission for Conciliation, Mediation and Arbitration (CCMA), but it seems he lost the case and he was never compensated for the injury he incurred at work. He walks with a limp. It always bothers me when kids tease him on the streets. I rarely speak to anyone about my father, for I am capable of injuring whoever happens to make a wrong remark about my father. I do not allow room for that kind of conversation.

For all the mistakes he made while I was very little, I have forgiven my father. As a young man myself, I understand that it is not easy to be a man – especially a black man – in this country. And I, too, will have children in the future. I would not like my children to hold grudges against me. I love my father so much, and I know in my heart that he loves me too. He always gives me support and tries to make up for the turbulent times of the past. We now have a good relationship. In fact, I am more like my father than ever right now, and I use all the knowledge he taught me about politics to improve the lives of other people.

When my father lost his job, my mother officially became the sole breadwinner, as she had been before. She did everything she could to make sure that the family was taken care of. Her business selling goods was struggling. She quickly quit that job to work as a cleaner at the University of Pretoria, the university that would later reject my application.

I remember, one fateful winter morning, my father escorting my mom to work – it was still very dark, and as dangerous as it had been when I was three years old. They encountered a thug who wanted to rob them. My mother told me that the man had a gun, but that my father had fought him. Even with his disability, he had won the fight. My mom screamed for help at 4 a.m.; a dog from a nearby shack barked uncontrollably. My father was not easily intimidated, as most men were then, and many still are today. The attacker only managed to knock my father on the forehead with the butt of his 9 mm handgun. It seemed the gun was not loaded – which made sense, in the squatter camp.

My mother was terrified. She only whispered this to us: my father did not want us to know that he had been beaten by a gun, because he would appear weak. To be honest, though, my father was a hero.

Chapter 10
Teko, my hero

My mother was a devoted member of the ZCC, but I hated going to church with her because we had to wear jerseys all the time – even when it was very hot. And people always laughed at the ZCC members in our society. There was nothing I really liked about church, between drinking tea without sugar and the lousy sermons.

I then found myself a religion: I started playing soccer in my early teens. After collecting water from the JoJo tank with my crush, I changed my routine of hanging out with Mbuyelo or Success: they were TV people. I started to play soccer in the streets instead.

We mostly played *one pal* (one pole). We would put two stones across from each other, then form teams of three players each. We scored by hitting the stone. Then, the next team would get in. Sometimes, we would bet money. If we didn't have a soccer ball, it would not stop us from playing. We would make one using plastic bags, then continue with the game. The economic conditions in Mshongo were so bad that sometimes we even struggled to find a plastic bag in the streets.

I was fairly good at soccer and enjoyed myself on the streets. But there was one angry lady who always spoiled our fun. She was Bra Peter's neighbour; we called her Skobo (The Ugly One) because she was not that good-looking, and very stubborn on top of that. Once we kicked the ball into Skobo's yard, it was game over. She always complained '*Clili tsamayang ko grountung le etsa dust mo* (Clili, you guys should go and play in the soccer field).' Skobo had a point – our road was untarred, so we made a lot of dust when we played.

One of the players we used to play with on the streets played for the big teams at the soccer grounds. His name was Rodney Ramothwala, but we called him Rasta because he was dreadlocked. He always advised me to take my game to the grounds, where I could join my equals. I always brushed it off. Since I was only good in the streets, I was considered a coward for not going to the grounds. '*O le gwala, o tshaba dithaka tsao* (You are a coward, you can't even face your equals),' the others would usually say. I hated being called a coward, so I decided to go and face the big boys on the field.

Rasta took me to the grounds, which were about six hundred metres from my home, near the taxi rank where we used to get taxis to town. The grassless grounds were called *ko-Mmung* (in the soil).

The name of our soccer team was Young Tigers FC, but it was famously called Bushy after our coach Bushy Ma-kgopa. Most of the teams in Atteridgeville were called by the names of their owners. The biggest team, Blackburn Rovers, was known as God after their coach Godfrey. Ben-fica was known as Basona, Heroes was known as Masha, and Zebras as Master. Bro Master was also a policeman.

Rasta introduced me to Bushy, and I was accepted into his team. '*Kao san utle le copy ya stifakhate sao* (Bring a copy of your birth certificate tomorrow),' he said. I brought my certificate the next day, and was registered in our amateur league, known as the PFA (Phelindaba Football Association).

The great players in our league were Mzwakhe from Barcelona in Siyahlala; Mahlatsi, Jethro and Mgambu from God; Dada from Basona; Nghunghu from our team; and Nelson Ndhima from Jacaranda.

When I got to the grounds on my first day, I realised that positional football was very different from street soccer. It was much easier in the streets; following the rules was very hard. I ended up adapting to positional football, although I was not as good as I was on the streets. Soccer kept me away from many bad things. It kept me off the streets. After school, I would head straight to practice session. I think that is the genius of sports: it lets you escape from the temptations of this world.

ko-Mmung was surrounded by the Atteridgeville extensions in all directions: Extension 6 to the west, Extension 18 to the south, Extension 5 to the east and Extension 7 to the north, with Phomolong Clinic facing away from the grounds. There was some sewage running very close to the grounds. Once in a while, we would kick the ball into the sewage. The one who kicked it would be the one who had to fetch it.

We had two sets of kit. When we played at home, we wore all blue. When we played away, we wore all white.

Our coach Bushy taught us to take responsibility very early on in our lives. He would rotate the washing of the team's kit. That was genius: instead of being absent on match day, if it was your turn to wash the kit, you would be the first to arrive – with the kit for all the players.

I was now called by the name that Blacky had given me: Mkhalele. I played position 8 and Rasta played position 2. When he overlapped to pass the ball to the strikers, I would cover his position. I had learnt early in the game to cover my brother when he went out to attack.

Even though some of our teammates were already on recreational drugs, soccer kept us from experimenting. Bushy would constantly preach to us about the importance of physical fitness. Since we played on grassless grounds, I used Dickies flat shoes for practice. Then, when we went out to play our league matches on weekends at grounds that had a little bit of grass, like Masopha or Mbolekwa sports grounds, I would wear soccer boots. If you didn't train during the week, you wouldn't make it into the starting eleven on the weekend. It didn't matter who your daddy was – you had to prove yourself on the pitch and discipline yourself off the field.

I loved soccer very much, but I was a very emotional kid. I was an Orlando Pirates supporter. I told everyone that I would no longer support the team when it drew a game against Kaizer Chiefs. Pirates led the whole game 1–0. Shaun Bartlett scored a last-minute equaliser and my aunt, Conny Baloyi, laughed at me until I cried.

As much as I loved playing soccer, it was the lessons

that came with playing it that I enjoyed more: that, in life too, when you were running with the ball, somebody could give you the smallest shoulder push to throw you off balance and that, if you ran too fast, you would fall badly.

One day, during our league game against God in Mbolekwa, I went out for a tackle and fell very awkwardly. Normally, when you go out for a tackle like that one, you get up, dust yourself off and pretend you didn't feel any pain. You hide your pain in the same way as you hid the hurt and pain you experienced at home. But the tackle at Mbolekwa was unique. I broke my hand. I will never forget the pain I felt that day. It was second only to the pain I'd felt in Waterval township when I'd been circumcised.

My coach took me to Kalafong Hospital, which was very close to the grounds. We arrived just before 1 p.m. He called my mother, who arrived after twenty minutes. Then Bushy went home. My mother didn't really help to ease the pain I was feeling: '*U huhwa ngaku ulo dyisiwa magume, vona se u tshoveke na voko* (You are very rough. Look what you have done to yourself),' she said. We joined the queue and waited as a file was opened for me. We waited for three hours in the queue, since it was a weekend. I remember seeing all types of injuries, but mostly stabbings of people who had been drinking in the township. It was a horrible day.

My hand started to swell more and more by the minute. The pain was increasing. I wanted to shout for someone to attend to me, but the look in the eyes of a man who had been stabbed in the head kept me quiet.

He, too, wanted to be treated; so did the lady with the broken leg behind us.

The doctor saw us at about 5 p.m. and put a little rope around my neck in which I had to balance my hand. We were sent for X-rays, which confirmed that my hand was, indeed, broken. We returned to rejoin the queue. At 9 p.m., the doctor attended to us. 'We cannot operate on him since he has already eaten today,' he said. So, I was admitted to ward 8. I wanted to cry when my mom went home at about 10:30 p.m. *'Mhani ni la ku famba na nwina, ninge dyi, nita vuya na mpundu* (Mom, I want to go with you. I promise I won't eat. I will come back in the morning),' I cried. But the doctor said it wouldn't be possible.

I spent the night in ward 8. It was very cold: there were no blankets, and the sheets they gave us were very thin. I needed boiling water to make coffee and keep myself warm and ease the pain I was feeling. But I had to wait, because the nurses were 'busy' and patients were not allowed in the kitchen.

The patient in the bed next to mine talked about his time there. He told me about the attitude of the nurses and the lack of infrastructure, proper management and dedicated staff. *'A bare tshware pila mo spetlele se, if nne kena le chelete, nkebe ke ile ko private* (The services in here are very poor. If I could afford it, I would have gone to a private hospital),' he said. Health-care issues at Kalafong also added to my pains.

I went for surgery the following day. They drugged me; all I remember is waking up with a cast on my hand.

I was discharged the following Monday. My mother came to fetch me. At school, they called me Mr Ice Cream. My peers would freely sign their autographs on my cast. I wore that thing for four weeks. It seemed that every time I went to hospital, I would need four weeks to recover.

After recovering, I was determined to get back onto the field. My hopes were always high: scouts from the local team of SuperSport United would come and watch us when we played at Makhaza sports grounds.

I was very happy when I heard that Thabiso Nkoana had been promoted to SuperSport United's senior team. 'Jethro', as we affectionately knew him, was very talented, and played for God. Even though we were never team-mates, and I didn't know him personally, I remember rubbing shoulders with him. He was very popular in the league. When I watched him play on television, I saw my dreams in the flesh and marvelled at the fact that dreams do come true. Thabiso's success made me determined to become a professional player. After I'd come back from my injury, our coach organised a game against the SuperSport United development side. I was anxious that day – it would be my first time playing at Super Stadium.

Super Stadium was in the centre of Atteridgeville, on the corner of Hlahla and Maunde streets. The stadium was very close to the ZCC that my mother used to attend. Next to Super was Atteridgeville police station and community hall. The stadium was used as a home ground of the Premier Soccer League (PSL) clubs Mamelodi Sundowns and SuperSport United. SuperSport United, affectionately known as *Matsatsantsa a Pitori*, was a local team. Super Stadium's name was changed to Lucas Moripe Stadium in 2010, honouring the legendary local soccer player Lucas 'Masterpieces' Moripe, the father of the notorious William 'Mashobane' Mbatha.

When our coach organised the game, I remembered the first time I had gone to watch a football match at Super Stadium, before it was called Lucas Moripe. Mr Mabasa had given us at school free tickets to go and watch Bafana Bafana play against Equatorial Guinea in the AFCON (Africa Cup of Nations) qualifiers. My mother had always discouraged me from going to the stadium. She would always tell me about the 2001 Ellis Park stampede that saw forty-three people crushed to death. But I now know the reason why she did not allow me to go to the stadium: she didn't have money for the tickets.

Teko Modise was the biggest guy in South African football. Every kid in the township idolised Teko. And, because I lacked a perfect male role model in my household, Teko became my role model. As I was walking from my home to the stadium, which was about a kilometre and a half away, to watch that first game, I was very happy that I was finally going to see in the flesh the people I had seen on TV. When I got to the stadium, I was so fascinated to see Teko Modise that it was almost like a dream. I didn't really focus on other players like Siphiwe Tshabalala or Itumeleng Khune – my eyes were glued to Teko. As usual, Bafana didn't win that game. And I know that not everything can be about race in this country, but, since most black guys play soccer, we experience the same black experience with Bafana – that is, the pain and suffering. (As a black person, when you get to the stadium you are already depressed, whereas, for white folks, it's all about joy and braaiing. I was to witness this a decade later when I got to university, since I stayed near to Ellis Park Stadium. White people would always leave smiling on the weekends, after a Springboks game. It was as if Bafana and the Springboks represented the lives of blacks and whites in this country.) After that Bafana game, I waited for the team to go out to their buses. I yelled to Teko, because the security guards wouldn't allow me to go near the players. I remember Teko waving at me and being filled with joy. That memory has stayed with me.

So, when our coach organised the game against Super-Sport, I wondered – would I be standing where Teko Modise had once played? I didn't know how familiar with the grass I was going to become.

Upon our arrival at the stadium, the first thing I saw was a huge SuperSport United logo on the door of the changing room. We were instructed to go into the visitors' changing room, which faced the home ground changing room. The changing room floor was overly polished, as if they wanted us to slip and fall. There were big mirrors near the door and on the side was a partition that led to the showering booths. We sat down on the dressing room benches, which had built-in fittings designed for each player. In each panel was a coat hanger. We put our white kit there. They served us some refreshments. This made us feel important and set high standards for us. While we were eating, Bushy stood in front of a board that was similar to our chalkboard in Masizane. The coach's tactics were on the board. Bushy stood in front of us like Mr Ngobeni did when he taught us mathematics. 'Mkhalele, we are in the future, my boy,' he said, looking straight into my eyes. All the guys laughed. It was a very good day for all of us. We spent most of the time laughing and teasing one another before we walked out onto the field.

You begin football games in the mind – by manipulating your opponents, playing mind games. As we walked out of the dressing room and met with our opponents in the tunnel leading to the pitch, those SuperSport boys were singing and doing everything they could to annoy and disrupt us. Their tactics worked – we were all anxious. We finally got onto the field and walked out of the tunnel through which my hero Teko had once passed.

The field at Super was very big. Those SuperSport boys outran us. They attacked us mostly from the flank, where Rasta and I played. During the game, I imagined what I might become. I imagined myself playing in the PSL and scoring the winning goal of the tournament. Playing on the same pitch that Teko Modise had played on, I was forced to raise my hopes.

Since we were all anxious, our team ended up losing the game 10–0. That was the biggest score margin I have ever experienced on the losing side. But we didn't care, because we were playing at a real stadium – unlike where we played on the weekends, on the dusty fields of Mmung, Masopha, Makhaza and Mbolekwa sports grounds.

After the game, we went back to the dressing room and were allowed to take showers. It was the first time I'd come back from a soccer match and didn't have to take a bath. And I smelled nice.

To be honest, I ended up quitting soccer when I was sixteen because I was not that good. I was just an average player. But I believed that, one day, I would live to play in the PSL and my parents would watch me on TV with great pride, just as Thabiso's parents watched their son. As a kid, there were many things I thought I could do, but could not. As I experienced with soccer, growing up as a born-free I was told that there were a lot of things I could access – education, shelter, even food, some-times.

But I found them hard to attain.

Chapter 11
Let's go to church

When I stopped playing soccer, I was always bored at home. Seeing this, my sisters tried to persuade me to go to their new church. My sisters loved church – they had left the ZCC to join the Pentecostal church. As new recruits, they threw Jesus at everyone.

'*Clili swilava hi ya kerekeni nwana mhani* (Clili, you must join us at church),' Tsakani would say. They told me that I had to repent, and that all my sins would be forgiven. Sometimes, their pastor would visit our home. Pastor Nathi would also tell me to visit their church.

I always turned them down. But whenever they mentioned church, I would grab the Bible and read it on my own. It always went straight to my heart, because I read it in my home language. Reading stories such as that of Job made me question the Bible, though, because I just never believed such things had ever happened. (I was a very stubborn and argumentative child. Such qualities would often land me whippings from the older guys in the streets.) But, since stopping soccer, I no longer had an excuse. I decided I would visit once, just so they would leave me alone.

On Sunday 23 May 2010, I went to His Rest Christian

Fellowship church for the first time. His Rest was a typical Bazalwane (born-again Christian) church, characterised by dancing, screaming and shouting, followed by the powerful voice of the pastor. I would watch the pastor jumping up and down and shouting as he preached, with the congregation jumping and shouting behind him, their souls and bodies devoted to singing and praying.

On that first day, I knew I would be going back. His Rest erased all the stigma I'd previously had about church. We did not have to wear jerseys (you wore whatever you wanted), there was no tea (which I didn't enjoy drinking without sugar), and the pastor spoke English.

I was hooked.

The church was based at Ramushu Hall. The Atteridgeville municipal offices, community hall, police station, Engen garage and Lucas Moripe Stadium formed a complex on the eastern side of the hall. Mbolekwa Sports Grounds and the Atteridgeville train station lay to the west. Ramushu Street stretched to the south. To the north of Ramushu Hall was the Ramsquare Café nightclub, owned by Lucas Moripe's son 'Mashobane'. When the young men and women were going home to rest after an all-night dance, we would be going to church.

There was a little stage inside the hall. When you walked in, you felt like you were going to a concert to see a live performance. The ushers stood like bouncers in a club. The difference was that they smiled and were mostly ladies.

On my first day at His Rest, Pastor Nathi was the MC.

'Can I see the first-time visitors?' he asked, and I raised my hand.

I was the only first-time visitor that day: His Rest was a small and intimate church and, since winter was approaching, there were a lot of empty seats. I guess the Lord was not good when it was cold. After Pastor Nathi prayed for me, the whole congregation clapped hands for me.

'Welcome to His Rest Christian Fellowship, my brother. We are under the leadership of Pastor David and Florence Khoza,' the pastor said. 'The vision of the church is to be like Christ and make his rest our dwelling place, with the scripture reference from Isaiah 11:10.'

Then the service continued.

The only problem I had with His Rest was the dancing part. I looked around. Everyone was dancing and having the time of their lives. This was a challenge for me: I could not dance. I could not sing either, and I did not know the lyrics to most of the songs, but that part I would not worry about because they had a giant screen displaying the lyrics. I tried to practise the dance moves that were popular at that time, but I could not execute my dance moves properly. I was always off the beat and my embarrassment at my inexperience showed.

They took an offering and I felt bad because I didn't have anything in my pocket. After the offering, they continued with the singing. The singing this time was better. People were no longer dancing, but they were singing slowly, and others began crying. Again, I felt bad because I was not crying and I was not as focused as everybody else was. The awkward singing quickly passed and the senior pastor, David Khoza, took to the podium and started preaching. There were some ladies who were shouting 'Amen, pastor!' as Pastor Khoza was preaching. Pastor Khoza was a very powerful preacher. I felt compelled by the sound of his speech.

The teachings and precepts of Jesus Christ spoke to me directly, and stirred and awakened something in me – my responsibilities to myself and to others. A belief that I am my brother's keeper, my sister's keeper. I think about the destiny of reaching heaven, where we will be welcomed by angels and God with a handshake for a job well done . . . as long as we did His job well here on earth, which is to feed and clothe the poor, love our neighbours as we love ourselves, and seek His kingdom and all its righteousness. From that service onwards, I started to have more respect for most people who represented religion.

My sister Tsakani played a huge role in making sure that I settled in well at His Rest. She was big on evangelism. She would team up with another pastor in the church, Clifford Khomelene, who was a policeman by profession. They simply called him Pastor Cliff. Tsakani and Pastor Cliff would go out and preach to the people in the streets.

There was another pastor who attended church with us. He was called Pastor Dilebo. He was a sweet Tswana man. He used to attend the services with his three children and his wife. The leadership of the church included

Mrs Tefo and a certain couple, Elias and Sarah Mudzunga. The church held its annual conference around 1 August, the birthday of His Rest. All this information was given to me after church when I went to the visitors' room.

As I got used to going to church, I started noticing the different personalities of the people who attended. Some danced as if they were in a nightclub. After all, there were similarities between the church-goers and the young people I would see leaving the nightclubs on Sunday mornings. Some just stood there, unshakeable, as if they were in the military. I was always fascinated by those who stood still because, deep down, I envied their self-control. So, I ended up deciding to be part of them.

When I became a military guy at church, I got comfortable, and started looking forward to Sundays – now, I did not have to dance. I could just stand there and watch everyone; when a good song played, I could just lift my hand up towards the sky as if the Holy Spirit was talking to me.

Our lady pastor – we called her Mmamoruti – would organise the choir. She was married to the senior pastor. She didn't take any nonsense; some members were suspended if they acted inappropriately or broke church rules or biblical commandments. The ladies in the choir usually dressed in black and white, and the guys dressed in a similar way. They sang songs mostly from the popular gospel group Joyous Celebration. My favourite song was *Le Jeso Nka ya kae* (With Jesus, I can do all things) by Keke Phoofolo, another popular gospel singer.

My favourite part was when Pastor Nathi, the usual

MC, would say, 'Go to two or three people and hug them and tell them that they look better than they did the last time you saw them.' I would be so glad, because you got to hug beautiful women whom you would probably never get to hug under different circumstances. The women of His Rest were so beautiful. They exposed their cleavages and wore tight clothes that left little to the imagination. I would usually get about ten hugs per Sunday . . .

Chapter 12

Clinton is born again in Atteridgeville

Since I was very consistent in attending church, I grew very quickly in the spirit. After a few months, I was officially baptised in Matshiga swimming pool just behind Lucas Moripe Stadium.

On the morning of 3 November 2010, I woke up very early to join the other young people from our church. Among them were Mashudu Motau, Lethabo Tshwane, Paballo and Seipati Molautsi, and Duduzile and Precious Tshivhandekano.

Pastor Cliff and Pastor Nathi were the ones in charge of the religious ritual. I got into the swimming pool and both men grabbed me and dunked my whole body and took me out after a few seconds. This symbolised that I had been born again. Pastor Khoza gave us a sermon later in the swimming pool. He even taught us how to pray in tongues. It is very difficult to explain, but yea, we were speaking in some heavenly language.

After that, I thought to myself, *The best decision I ever made was to accept Jesus Christ as my Lord and Saviour.* At a critical point in my life – a time when I think I would have started experimenting with alcohol or drugs to seek solace from my struggles, just like most kids around me – I was introduced to Christ.

From that point, I was very enthusiastic about Jesus. I studied the Bible fiercely. I could quote everything, from Genesis to Revelations. And since politics was the centrepiece of Jesus' story, I regarded him as one of the most skilful politicians in history. I liked how he engaged with some of the greatest minds of his generation and always won. Everything I did was Jesus-related.

Monday was prayer at Ma-Jerry's place in house number 60 Nomaziko Street, in the new settlement that was very close to my uncle's house in Selbourne Side. Tuesday was home-visit prayer to any church member who would request such a prayer. Wednesday was cell group. We used to attend home cell at Pastor Cliff's house in Extension 6, since he lived near to us, to discuss Pastor Khoza's sermon. Those who stayed in Oud Stad attended at Sister Joice's home. Those who stayed in Black Rock attended at Pastor Dilebo's or Mrs Tefo's house at 24 Madiba Street. Mrs Tefo had a big upstairs area. When you stood at the corner of Sekhu and Maunde streets, and looked at the hill towards Laudium, you could see Mrs Tefo's house; when you looked towards town, you could see the Lucas Moripe Stadium. Mrs Tefo was a lecturer at the University of South Africa.

Thursday was a day off. Friday was youth meeting. In these meetings, we met with different types of young people from different homes in Atteridgeville. We would usually choose a topic and invite one of the elders in the church to come and help us as we discussed it. There is one guy who changed my life at our youth meetings.

His name was Jerry Siwelo and I could talk all day about him. He is the one who recruited my sisters to church.

At one of our meetings, he asked me whether I would be interested in him mentoring me. I gladly accepted the offer. He bought me a leather jacket. It looked very nice on me. During our sessions at his house, we talked about everything, from finances to public speaking to Christian dating. Jerry was very good-looking and was good with women. All the girls liked him; he would often give me some tips.

Jerry taught me how to master public speaking. He would say, 'Public speaking is very important in your life. Without it, you cannot make it, Clinton.' A few years later, I found Jerry's words to be true. Public speaking enhances your confidence and is also a great asset in the corporate environment. Jerry used to give me transcripts of Obama's speeches so that I could practise. People used to call him The Young Obama.

In the garage where we used to host our Monday prayers, Jerry would set the chairs up in such a way that I would address those who attended. I struggled to make eye contact at first, but, as our meetings progressed, I improved.

Jerry excelled in all the areas he trained me in, and also played drums for the choir at church. But I was jobless at church. I didn't know how to sing or dance or play any instruments. My dancing skills had not improved; neither had my singing skills. So, I ended up taking the spot of cameraman. Jerry was smart – he would usually advise me to watch the people who spoke in church: '*Ejo u checker munhu loyi a tekaku* offering *or loyi a endlaku ti* announcements, then *u teka ti* techniques *ta vona* (Dude, pay attention to the person who speaks before taking the offerings, or the one who makes announcements, so you can improve your public speaking skills).'

I remember, once, we went to Turfloop in Limpopo to attend the wedding of a couple in our church. It was Jimmy and Comfort Malemela's wedding. I asked the couple if I could give a speech, and they both agreed. This was great, since they were not even family members. Jerry promised that he would scrutinise my speech. After the speech, in Mankweng Community Hall, Jerry was very impressed.

Soon after the wedding, Jerry completed his studies at Milpark Business School. He invited me to the graduation ceremony, saying, '*Ejo nivala ku u languta ti* guest speakers *da ka ti* graduations *and u* adopter style (I want you pay attention to the guest speakers at the ceremony).'

We went to the event with Florence Khoza, our pastor, who was also Jerry's aunt – Pastor David Khoza and Jerry's father were blood brothers. We travelled to Centurion in her Toyota Hilux and, after a few minutes searching for a place to park, we arrived at the venue at about 6 p.m.

We walked up to the second floor, to the hall where the ceremony would be held. We sat in the third row, me between Florence and Jerry. Jerry was then called and asked to put on in his graduation gown. As he walked out, the programme of the ceremony started.

They called out the guest speaker for the day. I was very attentive to him – that was the main reason Jerry had invited me. He spoke for about an hour, then the students started to queue at the side of the hall, not far away from where we sat. They waited for about twenty minutes, all dressed up and ready to ascend the stage.

Their names were called out in alphabetical order. As the announcer said, 'Jerry Godfrey Siwelo,' he walked up to the podium. Florence and I gave him a huge shout as they gave him some rolled-up paper. Florence made some strange, funny sounds; the whole hall erupted in laughter and clapped once again as the cameras flashed at Jerry's face from different angles. After the ceremony, Jerry found us in the crowd. We went to the first floor and took photos.

We left the venue and went to the Spur, a restaurant not very far from the venue, to celebrate his graduation. It was the first time I had been to a fancy restaurant. I felt very out of place. We chose a table near the entrance. After we had been sitting there for a couple of minutes, a waitress brought us the menu. I looked at the menu and was perplexed. The only thing I knew on that menu was a burger. Jerry ordered some complicated stuff while I was still studying the menu. Florence quickly took it from me and said, '*He baba, u dya yini?* (Hey man, what are you having?)' Florence didn't behave like a typical lady pastor. She was strict, yet lovable and playful. I ended up hitting her with, 'I am going have what he is having,' pointing at Jerry.

Florence was fond of me. She had formed a gospel choir called Atterise (Atteridgeville arise), which was a separate choir from the one in our church. Atterise had the most talented gospel singers in Atteridgeville. They released their first album in 2012. She also wanted to launch a magazine for Atterise. She chose me, Mashudu Motau and Precious Tshivhandakano as its editors. We would meet at her house at 3 Walter Siqolo Street, close to the Saulsville Arena, to discuss what the magazine would look like.

Florence also owned a media company called Flojo Entertainment. She was very well connected. She was friends with most members of Joyous Celebration, including Bheka Mthethwa, Xolani Mdlalose and founder Lindelani Mkhize. She later became the manager of Khaya Mthethwa, the first black person to win the singing competition known as Idols South Africa.

Soon after the graduations, Jerry took me to attend a workshop at Hatfield Christian Church in Waterkloof Glen, Pretoria East. The church was just behind the Menlyn Park Shopping Centre.

The church didn't look like ours. Their structure looked like an office complex. I marvelled at how big it was. As we got to the gate, we were greeted by well-lit church signs and information booths. As Jerry drove his car inside, I asked, '*He mmuna, ha ha ri a ndeni ka kreke?* (Hey man, are we still on the church premises?)'

He laughed: '*Jah, di kreke yi kulu mmuna* (Yes, this church is big, man).'

After a long drive, we finally got to the parking lot.

Two white girls came and greeted us. It looked like they had known Jerry for a long time. We walked into a mall-like courtyard. As we got in, we passed a huge and spacious auditorium, with comfortable theatre seating, a large stage and a minimum of white Jesus portraits. We were served with refreshments. Jerry was having a serious conversation with a white guy who looked to be the organiser of the workshop, while I was having a conversation with one of the white girls whom Jerry had left me with.

'Wow, your church is big, hey,' I said.

'Yeah, it is, hey.'

We chatted for a while, but our conversation didn't really go anywhere. Shortly after that, we walked into the small auditorium and listened to the man who had been talking to Jerry. The meeting flew, and we left. Jerry took me back home at about 10:30 p.m. In the morning I was left with only the memories. I often heard megachurch pastors saying that they were 'not just playing church' at Hatfield Christian Church. I couldn't agree more. The church itself – its size, pastor, programmes and reputation – really settled that point.

Jerry had truly broadened my world.

Coming back to His Rest, I felt like our God was very small. The God of Hatfield Church was the God of white people. It was a prosperous God. The God of His Rest was the God of black people. It was a poor God, and a very funny one.

Back at our little church, Saturday was another day off and Sunday was a normal church service. At His Rest,

113

we would usually have fasting and prayer at the beginning of the year. Fasting was both very hard and very easy for most of us, because at home there would be nothing in the fridge – if we had a fridge. Nobody fasted like me and my sister Tsakani.

In January 2011, we were fasting for twenty-one days, after the biblical Daniel, who fasted for that long. I joined the guys for fasting, as usual. I drank water, only to keep myself going. The fasting was difficult for us, because we stayed a bit far from church. I would travel one kilometre to school. After school, I would travel another kilometre and a half by taxi. If I had failed to save money for transport, I would walk that distance to have money for the offering at church. The temptations during breaktime at school were real. But at home it was worse, because Akani would usually break her fast. I would envy her as she ate with Mom and Dad in front of us.

I wanted to break my fast, but one guy from church, Katlego Chiloane, said to me, '*He mmuna oska jah, otla ja lenyalo la gao* one day (Hey, man, don't break your fast. You might jeopardise your chances of getting married).' This impressed Pastor Khoza, who was very close to us as we were talking. Katlego's remarks were the greatest blackmail – as young men at His Rest, the only thing that we were looking forward to, other than the coming of Jesus, was getting married. Getting married was the greatest achievement. I remember Pastor Khoza hosting a dating and relationships seminar during that period at Makgatho Primary School, which was very close to the Christ-centred Christian Church. During that seminar,

'When you date, inform us,' 'Don't date when you are still in high school,' and 'No sex before marriage,' were all preached with great passion. These principles were difficult to follow for most people, but I think the church's ideas about dating and sexuality still influence me. They are excellent principles.

I ended up breaking the fast on my nineteenth day, two days away from reaching Daniel's milestone. I came back home looking very weak. Upon seeing me, my mom cooked soft porridge and said, '*Nwananga dyana, phela se ulo sala hi nhloko, vatswatsi ava swi endli leswi, hambi kona naku chava nwananga* (My son, let me prepare food for you, because you are weak. I admire you – even the adults fail to fast).'

My mother didn't have a problem with us attending His Rest: as long as we were in church, it was fine with her. In fact, it was we who had a problem with her. We thought our church was better, and our God was better. We thought she was in the darkness at the ZCC. I had started to develop a type of hatred for my parents, the people who had brought me into this world. I no longer joined my father at his rituals of speaking to the ancestors. '*Mi ta ya tiheleni hi swileswi swa nwina, Jeso wa vuya* (You will go to hell with this crap of yours. Jesus is coming back),' I would tell him.

Now that I think about these things with a clearer mind, it always raises my eyebrows that, when the Chinese people seek the path of Buddha or the Indians worship their Hindu deities, it is considered idolatry; when the Muslims worship Allah, they are terrorists; when the

115

Africans worship their ancestors, it is considered demonic; and when modern-day Africans worship Lekganyane, it is also considered idolatry. But when the white people worship Jesus, it's pure common sense – you know, practical stuff! Allow me to tell you something, though: all these things are superstitions – just a bunch of adults hallucinating.

I was very committed to church services and Pastor David Khoza was very impressed with how I followed the church's rules. I don't know if it was Pastor Khoza's liking for me that made his wife like me, or whether it was his wife's liking for me that made Pastor Khoza like me, or Jerry's mentoring me. One thing I know is that the Khozas liked me.

They made me a youth leader. I was doing very well in my sessions with Jerry. On Sundays, they would make me an MC. When I had the mic, I would turn the church upside down: I would touch lives with my humorous delivery. And most people loved me. I remember, once, as I was leaving the church building, shaking hands and greeting people, one lady, who was almost the same age as my grandmother, came to me and said, 'You know, some of us, when we come to church, we come bearing pain in our hearts, so when you make all those jokes, you heal us. You are really a blessing, boy.' She said this while giving me a hug. I will never forget her.

Deeply involved in the things of church, I started observing some subtle behaviours. I had always asked myself a question: why do pastors' children turn out to be drunkards, or turn out to be the opposite of their parents? The answer to that question lay in the concept of choice. I learnt that life really was a series of choices. When you wake up in the morning, you have a choice. You have a choice whether to get out of bed or not, whether to take a bath or not, whether to go to school or not, whether to participate or not. Nobody can make you decide what you want to do. I observed that, no matter how hard parents would hit their children, they could never make them what they did not want to be. They could only guide them; the choice would always remain in the children's hands. This was true for me.

I was a good son. At least, I would like to think so. I had the time of my life at His Rest. But I was sad when our pastor died. In a tragic event, our pastor, David Khoza, was murdered in his house. I had always had a problem with black top achievers who distanced themselves from the 'hood. Once people got educated, they left the 'hood and went to stay in the suburbs and never came back to encourage or support others financially. Pastor Khoza had chosen to stay. Pastor Khoza had graduated from the University of Pretoria as an electrical engineer. He was the first black engineer employed by Denel Dynamics, which grew out of missile research, design and development. He had dedicated his life to serving the community that loved and needed him. After his death, I understood why people moved to the suburbs. As a community, we had a tendency to kill useful people then act betrayed when people like them moved to the suburbs.

Pastor Cliff then took over as a senior pastor. Other than that, His Rest was a refuge for me. We were poor;

they preached to us that we were the most blessed people on earth. The little that I got for school lunch, I would offer on Sundays. They preached that we should store our treasures in heaven, where we were ultimately going. But I think the church was wrong in this case. I think it's a bad thing for people who struggle financially to donate a lot of money to the church.

Chapter 13

Saulridge: Skolo sa
Bob Mabena

To go back a few years, I completed primary school in 2007 and started at Saulridge High School in 2008. The name Saulridge was basically a combination of Saulsville and Atteridgeville, and referred to the location of the school. It was situated in Matebeleng section, where the two townships converged, separated by a single street (Sekhu Street). The school was between the Saulsville train station and Ga-Mothakga Resort. Ga-Mothakga Resort was the site of the *SS Mendi* memorial tombstone, which paid tribute to the soldiers who died when the *SS Mendi* sank during World War I. Ga-Mothakga and Saulridge were separated by a bridge, under which the trains from the Saulsville station travelled. Our fellow learners from Lotus Gardens travelled over the bridge on Tlou Street, the entrance to Atteridgeville from Church Street.

I had joined my sisters at Saulridge. In the mornings, I would wait for them to bath while watching Leanne Manas and Vuyo Mbuli on SABC 2's *Morning Live* on our black-and-white TV. I would watch the time pass on the top corner of the screen, waiting for Akani to finish bathing since I was the youngest. My sisters would usually leave me behind. When they had left, I would steal Akani's

Ponds cream and apply it to my face so I would look lighter. I would look so pale, the guys would tease me at school. But other female classmates also applied creams to look like white people.

Our school had two entry points, one in Moroe Street and a smaller one in Sekhu Street. The small gate close to the caretaker's house would usually be closed. In the morning, I went through a small gate to the markets at Saulsville station to buy *vetkoek* ('fat cakes') called *magwinya*. Upon my return, I would sometimes find the small gate closed. Then, I would have make my way to the main entrance to the school in Moroe Street. But this would cause a delay. If I walked in late, I would find Mr Poo (a real Tswana surname) standing at the gate. He would whip latecomers' buttocks using a length of red plumbing tube. It didn't matter that I had dropped my school bag in the classroom earlier.

After getting my whipping, I would make my way into the school by walking about fifty metres on a small road-way that led to the administration offices. Instead of going to the teachers' parking lot, I would keep left and make my way between two blocks – one for computers, and the other for the library. I would finally pass the stinking toilets then go to room number three, my classroom. Our classroom was complete with a chalkboard, desks and chairs. Most of the time, we would find that vandals had broken the doors, windows and plugs, and had stripped the building of its fittings or electrical connections.

Our school represented the good and the bad of society.

We had young thugs and young pastors. In the toilets, you would sometimes get mugged. We had girls who dated big boys who had money. Those big boys who had money were taxi drivers.

In front of our block (rooms 1–4) was an open space where we usually assembled on Mondays and Fridays. Our assembly point was bound by the toilets to the west and the laboratory to the east. Our class was to the north. Mr Modise was the conductor at assembly; we sang gospel songs and waited for a Christian preacher to deliver a short sermon. In so doing, the school was forcing Christianity down our throats while we were still young. My favourite was when we gathered at assembly on Fridays. One guy would go to assembly and start dancing. Our school principal, Moagi Mangena, would laugh. That is the only time you would see Mr Mangena laughing. (Mr Mangena had a very strong presence. After the bell had rung, learners had a tendency not to go back to class. But when Mr Mangena walked out, smoking his cigarette, everyone would run into the classrooms.)

After the singing and prayers, Mr Mangena would stand in front of us, without a lectern in front of him, and eloquently address us. The whole school would be quiet and listen to the state of the school, which was always in bad shape. After hearing the depressing facts such as the burglary during the weekend, poor performance by learners, or teenage pregnancy in the school, he would motivate us with his one signature line: '*Se ke skolo sa Bob Mabena* (This is Bob Mabena's alma mater).' He was very proud of Bob Mabena. Bob Mabena was a very popular radio DJ for Khaya FM. Mr Mangena himself had taught Bob Mabena mathematics in the very same school, a fact he always reminded us about. And then he would dismiss the assembly and walk to his office. On his way, he would pass the woodwork centre where Mr Nyathi (the Technology teacher) was stationed. Before I enrolled at the school, Mr Nyathi had been stationed at the woodwork building after a stampede in which students had attacked him. I am told that he was standing in the doorway refusing to let the learners leave after school. They then pushed and injured him.

In Grade 8, I met learners from other primary schools such as Phuthaditshaba, Mahlahle, Bathokwa, Banareng, and J.J. De Jong. Among them, I was a fairly cool kid; the struggles at Masizane had prepared me to stand up for myself. I was not separated from my friend Success Nobela – we attended the same class in room 3. But Katlego Ngobeni was in room 1. We had twin sisters in our class. Their names were Charmaine and Charlotte Valoi. I was making all the jokes, clowning around and making fun of other learners. I was very mischievous, but I was also a bit book smart, so the teachers didn't know what to do with me. My sister Tsakani was the smartest kid in our family, though. I always looked up to her. She helped me with my homework. The teachers at Saulridge who had taught her always expressed their disappointment in me. 'Clinton, you are not as smart as your sister,' Mr Mashele would say.

Our class teacher was Mr Seema and he taught us English. He liked to say *scientia potentia est*, which is Latin for 'knowledge is power'. *Scientia potentia est* was also our school motto. The other subjects were vernacular (mine was Xitsonga), Technology, Geography, Mathematics, Social Science, Natural Science, and Arts and Culture. My favourite subject was Life Orientation. Life Orientation was not really a subject – it was time for us to play. We would come to school with casual clothes in our bags. During Life Orientation period, we would go and change in the toilets. Our toilets were dangerous, though – on my first day I got robbed by one of those young thugs we had in the school. They took my lunch money. The toilets were filthy. I never used the toilets for their purpose at school, but I did clean them, when it was our week to clean them. Since our school had twenty-four classrooms, each week one class would be required to clean the toilets. We also cleaned our own classrooms. During the week, we would usually sweep; on Fridays, the boys would wash the windows using newspapers and the girls would come up with their *skoropos* (mopping cloths) and mop and polish the floor. We would have contributed money to buy the polish.

Unused desks, plastic bags and papers littered our little schoolyard. Some teachers were also taxi drivers, and came to teach in their own time. Some never came to class, to a point where we forgot that they taught us.

Teenage pregnancy was growing exponentially at our school. Our sports HOD, Mr Latakgomo, once confided in me that he had a feeling that the school was going back to its original name of Batswadi (meaning 'parents') – Saulridge was initially called Batswadi Secondary School back in the eighties, for it was one of the few schools that accommodated students who were pregnant during that time.

I remember Faith Molefe, who dropped out in Grade 8 to nurse her newborn baby. Her husband was working, so everything was fine – he was providing for them. The problem came when he dumped her and she realised that, in order to get ahead, she needed matric. When she came back to school, they told her that she was very old; when she went to an ABET (Adult Basic Education and Training) institution, they told her she was still too young. Using my religious background, I quickly judged her in my mind. The church had taught us that it was a good idea for us young people to marry someone before deciding to have a baby with them. That would ensure that the child would grow up in a healthy family, and the chances of that child succeeding would also increase.

Our school president was Jerry Siwelo, my mentor. He would lead the Bible study group during breaktime.

At school, I didn't hang around with my sisters. Tsakani's friends were Hilda Khosa and Thembi Masuluke and Akani's friends were Clementine Shingange and Lucia Ngobeni and Hitekani Maluleke. My friends at school were Success Nobela and Livewell Chauke. But, after school, I would walk back home with my sisters. They were good-looking, especially Tsakani. In the streets on our way back from school, the boys would frequently stop her. She didn't know how to turn them down. Sometimes she would break down. I remember one guy once stopped my sister, and she was not interested. He refused

124

to let her hand go and then he changed his tone. I was still young, I couldn't fight. I failed to defend my sister. I just stood there seeing the guy harassing my sister. He finally let her hand go. At home my mother always warned me against whistling to girls in the streets. She said a woman was supposed to be treated with respect. I would often overhear my mom giving my sisters lessons on what to expect from men. I would take notes. (And, in a few years' time, I would see my sisters graduating from these talks. My sister Tsakani got married to Saddam Ndlovu and together they have two beautiful baby girls, Kuhlula and Engetelo. They bought a house in Soshanguve, where they currently live.)

When I was in Grade 8, Akani was in Grade 10 and Tsakani was in Grade 12, also known as matric. This meant that Tsakani no longer wore the maroon-and-white dress known as *Tuniky*. She now wore a checked skirt and white buttoned shirt, with a tie that was similar to the skirt. When she completed matric, she gave Akani her skirt; that way, my mother wouldn't have to buy a new skirt when Akani reached matric. I felt sorry for Akani, because that was the story of her life from birth. She never got new clothes. As Tsakani grew, her clothes would be passed down to Akani – except on Christmas, because our parents would always buy us new clothes at Christmas. It was the birthday of a very special Man, so you had to look your best, in case He came back. The shoes we got for Christmas were always black. That way, we would use them for school when it reopened in January.

Tsakani completed matric and applied at the Tshwane University of Technology to study electrical engineering. She would only study for six months before dropping out – she didn't have money to pay for her tuition. Seeing our struggles at home, she applied for a post at Muelmed Mediclinic. I remember when she got accepted to be an auxiliary nurse. She came back home screaming: '*Va ni tekini!* (They have accepted my application!)' My mother gave her a big hug. I did the same thing. Akani also gave her a hug. Later in the evening, my father gave her R10 and was almost in tears.

After that, she was the only one who was making real money at home. The whole family became dependent on her. Tsakani was now paying what we call black tax, extra money that young, black professionals have to pay out in order to support their extended families. For Tsakani, it was not compulsory for her to pay the money. It was more like psychological blackmail. She grew up seeing the struggle at home, so she was forced to give back. As a general rule, you cannot live a luxurious life while your family suffers. But, a few years later, I saw some brave young men and women avoiding black tax and I didn't judge them.

In Grade 9, I was elected to be a class rep again – this time, with Charmaine Valoi, one of the twins. I knew I was cool because I owned a second-hand Motorola v360 cellphone that my uncle had given me. This was a very popular phone during that time. I used to watch a lot of pornographic videos on that phone. I am now sharing too much information. Where was I? Oh yes, the Mo-

126

torola. I loved my phone too much. One day I would have Beyoncé as my screensaver; the next, I would have Rihanna or Ciara. It just depended on how I felt.

When most of my classmates were still hooked on the popular social media application Mxit, I had moved to Facebook, which I thought was way cooler because I could make celebrities my 'friends'. My close friends also thought I was way cooler, since Facebook was more expensive and I was also friends with Lil Wayne, a popular American rapper. They thought I was a sophisticated guy. I would take messages from love-candy wrappers and make them my statuses.

It was during this time that I began to explore Pretoria properly. I would usually go to Saulsville station and ride a Metrorail train with my friends to town. We always put on our best clothes when we went to town, because that's where white people stayed. As a general rule, it is always safer to look presentable when you are going to meet 'serious people', you know. There were historic buildings everywhere I turned and statues of famous white men, standing so arrogantly. One statue in Church Square impressed me: a certain man named Paul Kruger, who had been the president of South Africa. With my friends, we would pose with Paul and his rifles. At school we were never taught about Paul, what he stood for and how he got to be president of the country – all that, we never knew. Although lessons about Paul Kruger would not have been ideal for a decolonised syllabus, I would have loved to have learnt about the man. We could not appreciate one another if we didn't know one another's histories.

I realised, then, that we didn't know one another's histories, despite them being painful. We did not even talk about history, which, in my opinion, was very dangerous. It's like we were sitting on a ticking time bomb, and we all knew it, but we never spoke about it. It would be only a matter of time before we stopped talking about everything – and, with the slightest of actions, the bomb would explode and kill us all. That's why I felt it was important for us to talk about Kruger, Verwoerd, Botha and all the others. And, similarly, the whites would be taught about Sekhukhune, Moshoeshoe, Hintsa and Nghunghunyane, and then we would appreciate one another.

Back to the streets of Pretoria: I would go window shopping at Sammy Marks Square and Tramshed with my friends. I loved Diesel, and everybody knew that. We never went to Marabi (short for Marabastad), because we thought it was too low-class for us. But, deep down, I knew that my mother bought us clothes from Marabi. Marabi became such a slum that, after a long period of time, the early residents of Atteridgeville were removed. Marabi was the equivalent of Small Street in Johannesburg, where they sold cheap merchandise.

I was no longer eating at the feeding scheme, because I thought it would make me unpopular. I came to learn that this was the paradox of a black man: the drive to look good while he is starving. Some pupils did not even know that I was staying in the squatter camp. This was very good for me: once they knew where I lived, they would stop taking me seriously. It was very difficult for me to hide this fact. As the American rapper Jay-Z once said, 'One of the reasons inequality gets so deep in [America] is that everyone wants to be rich. That's the American ideal. Poor people don't like talking about poverty because even though they might live in the projects surrounded by other poor people and have, like, ten dollars in the bank, they don't like to think of themselves as poor.'

As you already know, in every group of people there is always a class structure. And, even though a township is a poor place, the ones who lived in the shacks were the *really* poor ones. Next were those who lived in the RDP houses, then the four-room brick houses, then the new houses (bonds) and in the first class were the few who stayed in town. In retrospect, whenever I see someone who lives in an RDP house laughing at someone who lives in a shack, I do not know whether to laugh or cry.

While we walked around downtown Pretoria, we would always question our circumstances. Often, we would blame the white people for keeping us in the townships so that we could work for them. Success would always tell us, 'Gents, even though we may be living in the shacks, the shack is not the only thing, so we must get out and explore.' If there was one thing we never advised one another about, it was girls, because we were all girl-friendless. When I look at it now, I don't think it was important for us to have girlfriends anyway. But it did affect us, because it challenged our sense of masculinity. Our society perceives manhood by how many ladies you can bed. I think this is totally misguided.

During these times in town, we would take pictures in fancy places and post them on Facebook. People envied us. My Facebook page was very impressive. I ended up deleting my Facebook account, because each time I looked at my profile, it looked perfect. It didn't reflect my reality; I always put up nice things that made me look like a rich person when I was dirt poor. I figured out that, if I could check in somewhere in Japan while I was just chilling in my shack, it was time I stopped acting. One thing that had always fascinated me about Facebook was that I rarely saw my 'friends' post a status update about the problems they were going through. I asked myself, *Are we living in a perfect world where people don't have problems?* I concluded that Facebook was nothing but a contest of egos. My friends were disappointed when I deleted my account.

But back to Saulridge: our mathematics teacher, Mrs Moloto, was the real boss. She was one of the people who had migrated to Atteridgeville from Marabastad as a child. She used to tell us a bunch of stories about the time when they relocated. At the end of the year, we didn't write exams. We were assessed by tests known as CTAs (Common Tasks for Assessment), which were part of a compulsory, standardised education programme and were different from the testing criteria we were used to. The CTAs were the hardest. But, after completing Grade 9, you could decide to leave school without matriculation or to continue until Grade 12.

Chapter 14

Saulridge: Segregated school

When I completed Grade 9, I decided to continue with my studies in 2010. Grade 10 was the hardest grade in school. It was the class with the highest failure rate. We had nine Grade 10 classes. The most notorious class consisted of male learners only. Those guys in room 11 were really bad boys. They caused all kinds of trouble at school. It was well known that they carried dangerous weapons such as guns and knives to school. Everybody, including the teachers, was afraid of room 11.

Grade 10 was hard because it was a time of great transition in subjects. We had to choose streams from three distinct fields of study: the sciences, history and commerce. I chose the science stream, which consisted of Physical Science, Life Science, Mathematics, Geography, Life Orientation, Xitsonga as home language and English as first additional language. Success Nobela and Katlego Ngobeni, my homeboys from Masizane, also chose the science field.

In Grade 10, we met with the cream of the school, since the science class was considered a class for smart people. We met with guys like Amos Makgoba, Charlotte Valoi and Precious Modiba, who was sharp as a whip. I shared a desk with Floyd Maluleke, who stayed in Lotus Gardens. He was repeating the grade. Floyd gave me a lot of tips that got me through the year.

That year, they introduced awards ceremonies at school for top performers. The criterion was that you would get a certificate if you scored seventy per cent or above in a subject. By the end of the year, I managed to get three seventies and one eighty, but I was not awarded any certificates. As soon as I noticed that I had been robbed, I went to Mr Mangena's office. I found him sitting with Jabulani Mathibela, my Physical Science teacher. As soon as I started explaining my misfortune, I began to cry uncontrollably. Mr Mangena started to know me from that day as he issued me with some certificates.

Mr Mathibela was very fond of me: I was among the first-class students in his hierarchy. A former bodyguard to Nelson Mandela, he became a teacher and deputy principal at our school. He was very politically conscious; even though, politically, I was still an infant, he engaged me: 'The problem with your generation is that you are a drunk generation. You will notice that the only thing that you are looking forward to is booze, running after girls and making a quick buck.' By 'drunk' he meant affected by alcohol to the extent of losing control of one's faculties or behaviour. I agreed with him. 'Look, nice times have always been, and forever will be, there, so do not be concerned about that,' he added.

Mr Mathibela never treated me like a learner. He treated me like his son.

He used to express his disappointment with people who criticised Madiba. I totally sympathised with him. When Mandela was fighting for equal opportunities for every human being in this country, most people who criticised him were still in diapers – or were like me in the sense that they had not yet been born. Mandela was in prison for twenty-seven years. Some people who were not even twenty-seven were criticising him. He sold us a vision, but it was up to us whether we wanted to live up to it or not.

I would disagree with some of the statements that Mr Mathibela made, though. I told him that Mandela had walked so that we could run, but that we were failing because we had broken legs. Apartheid held us back, and the syllabuses did not change overnight – the reason why we fought so hard when I got to university. There was no way we could run with our broken legs. We had to fix them first. We were told to pull ourselves up by our own bootstraps – but what people failed to understand was that we did not have boots. With fewer resources for learning and fewer teachers, it was very possible for a school to achieve a matric pass rate of zero per cent as we observed around the country. I explained to Mr Mathibela that, with a zero per cent pass rate, no one was going to further their studies at an institution of higher learning.

In 2010, Mr Mathibela chose me and another nine learners to visit Pretoria Central Prison, also known as New Lock – a prison that had been an official site of capital punishment during the apartheid era. We visited the correctional service facility as part of the Take A Boy Child To Work programme. I was puzzled about why they took us to a prison. Maybe they did not want us to end up there. My confusion was cemented by the knowledge of where the girls were going. I knew they were going to Siemens, the cellphone company. I would have loved to have gone to a corporate company too.

We arrived at the prison, which was on the outskirts of Pretoria CBD, close to Weskoppies school on the exit towards Johannesburg. The complex was one of the largest in the country, up there with Pollsmoor in Cape Town, St Albans in Port Elizabeth, Durban–Westville and Johannesburg. At the time, I didn't know that this was the place where my heroes, Steve Biko and Solomon Mahlangu, had been killed. The countless gates, manned by warders with humungous and electronically controlled keys, delayed our arrival at our destination. We finally arrived at the administration building at about 9 a.m. A coloured warder welcomed us, and led us to a big boardroom that displayed the portrait of then minister of correctional services Nosiviwe Mapisa-Nqakula. We then sat down, all ten of us including Mr Mathibela. A white prisoner wearing white clothes prepared food for us. We were given a tour guide and who explained what was required of us when we visited different facilities.

'We have six correctional centres, including C-Max,' he said. He explained that the prisoners were kept in categories according to their offences, and dressed accordingly. The minimum-security prisoners wore white, like the guy who had prepared our food. Medium security wore orange and maximum security wore red.

From the boardroom, we started our tour of the prison. We started by walking in a partition of the male prison that had cells on the sides. As I looked inside one of the cells, I saw portraits of naked women on the walls. All the single-cell doors were open. The overwhelming number of prisoners were black people. There were a few whites, but no Indians. The cells were closed after a certain period, the same way we used to treat the chickens in the village. The warder started pushing the prisoners, who looked at us with mixed emotions. None of them qualified for C-Max. For our safety, we were restricted from visiting C-Max since it housed the highest-risk offenders. The warder told us that the notorious Ananias Mathe had escaped from there. He then added, 'Collen Chauke also escaped from this prison in 2001.' Everyone turned to me and we all laughed. As we moved from the cells to the woodwork centre, I still remember two of my schoolmates, Peter Maluleke and Botlhale Mashaba, showering the warder with a lot of questions. In the woodwork centre, we found some prisoners who were involved in prison labour. They were required to attend programmes aimed at rehabilitation. They indicated that they worked and got paid. This shocked me. The prisoners always looked like slaves, in my eyes. We didn't have time to go to the women's prison in the complex.

Our day at the prison was over.

I was impressed by how well known our teacher was. I thought he was the top dog, since most inmates knew him. But I later realised that our teacher's popularity among the prison inmates was an issue of concern, rather than a call for celebration. Knowing my teacher, obviously he was not impressed by the fact that most of the people he had once taught ended up in prison. It was a victory for the community when the criminals were put behind bars, but it was definitely a defeat for the parents when a child went to prison – and it was a great defeat for the country when most of its young people were put behind bars. I found a direct link between poverty and the situation. It was the same reason I called a shack my home; somewhere deep in my soul I knew that there was no difference between me and those prisoners. We were just locked in different prisons.

With hindsight, the visit to the prison gave me a sense that the hopes and desires of young black men would always be thwarted because very little is expected of them by authorities and members of their communities. The financial, political and social systems perpetually place them in compromised positions. Prison will forever be their home!

Shortly after our visit, we were sitting in Mr Mathibela's office, which had a giant photo of him standing next to the great Nelson Mandela. I was complaining about the fact that I stayed in a squatter camp. Angrily, he turned to me and said, 'Remember that it was hope that led the greatest generation in our country to march and protest in the streets of Sharpeville and Soweto for freedom's cause!' He cleared his throat and went on: 'It was hope that made Nelson Mandela to sit for twenty-seven years in jail for the same cause.' Then, he looked straight into my eyes. 'It is hope that will lead you to achieve whatever you put your mind to,' he reassured me. Mr Mathibela gave me not only education, but hope. But the hope he gave me would always be crushed by the subtle observations I made on a regular basis, especially when we visited good schools in town.

In primary school, I used to be number one in athletics, but the white kids would always outrun me. I decided to change sporting codes. I tried long jump, since there were few people doing it. Long jump proved to be a revelation. It even took me to an inter-schools athletics event at the Afrikaans high school in the eastern suburbs of Pretoria known as Hoërskool Waterkloof, not far away from Hatfield Christian Church. I still remember the school's motto, 'We build by faith'.

There were few black learners at that school. Leadership in every area – sporting, cultural and academic – was very important there. I could see it in the learners, who were all dressed in their beautiful blazers. I walked through well-maintained gardens, on green grass and weedless pavements. In the pure cleanliness of every block, I saw computer centres, a fully equipped kitchen, an art studio, pavilion and media centre. The classrooms had Internet access and were fitted with data projectors, and all teachers were equipped with computers. They had a big hall, which looked like it could hold the entire school. The school shop sold the official uniform. It also sold new and second-hand textbooks. When I walked past there, I remembered the state that we were in – I had to share a maths textbook with Floyd. I was shocked to see the beauty of Waterkloof High. I was used to seeing long buildings with colours painted on them running parallel to each other, from Nkandziyi to Masizane to Saulridge – to me, that was what a school represented.

Until I got to Waterkloof.

My biggest shock was when we got to the event itself. They had hockey fields, cricket fields, rugby fields, netball courts and swimming pools. Seeing the playing grounds, each of which was bigger than the yard of my school, it really hit me hard that, on paper, Saulridge and Waterkloof were considered 'normal public schools'. Yet the effects of apartheid's unequal education system could still be felt. I was very angry with the state – very resentful.

I noticed that there was a big difference between our schools and, as a result, a big difference between us as learners. When I tried to look for the main cause of this difference, its root, I found that it came from the fact that they had better resources for teaching and learning. This better explained the achievement gap between black students and white students. White people were privileged and black people were poor. So, poverty continued to have race. President Mbeki was spot-on when he declared that South Africa is 'a country of two nations' – one is white and wealthy, and the other is black and poor.

When I asked for directions from one of the Waterkloof learners, I was amazed by their eloquence and precision. On the field, they would outrun us. When we engaged in debates with them, we would always come second – not because they had better ideas, but because of their Model C accents. Our intelligence was measured by how well we were able to articulate our ideas in English. You know that people like to applaud eloquence more than content. There was nothing wrong with their expressing themselves and their views well, but we should also have paid attention to what they were saying.

I remember having an argument with Thabang Mala, who attended Pretoria Boys High. In the middle of our argument, he paused and said, 'Dude, I get the best education. My folks pay a lot of money for my education. So, trust me. I know better than you in this matter.' In a debate, when a man hits your insecurity, you have no choice but to concede and keep quiet. So, I immediately kept quiet.

Over and above the contents of books, the learners at schools like Waterkloof were well-equipped about life. Since they had competent and skilful teachers, they had been taught about the virtues of life and how to conduct themselves. They learnt about leadership from an early age, so they were poised, confident and charismatic – things we were never taught. Like how to carry ourselves as young professionals, and the implications of a firm handshake, strong eye contact and posture. They participated in spelling bees, debates and other useful activities. I mean, these activities may have seemed like they did not matter, but in the long run they did.

When we came back from Waterkloof, our Life Science teacher, Mrs Bopape, would teach us how to label the internal structure of a fish and a locust. I would sit there wondering how relevant that was to me.

Years after Bantu education, we were still trapped on the lonely island of inferior education. Some liked to talk about the victory of the class of 1976. To me, it was a victory that you could talk about, but not a victory that you could show me.

As young as I was, as young as our democracy, I had so many thoughts and unanswered questions running through my mind. I sensed a lot of optimism from young people like me. But the stations in which they were born did not allow them to express their full potential. It was easy for the short-sighted to say that, for young people, the sky was the limit. But to understand that phrase, somebody must first teach you.

Despite all the solid evidence that I would give to Mr Mathibela about the inequalities that existed in our societies, he would always push back with some strong statements. 'Well, Clinton,' he would say, 'we have all read about people who came from rough backgrounds. We have all heard about people who came from poor backgrounds and made it big. The greatest person ever to have lived on earth, Jesus Christ, came from a place that was not great. Someone once questioned, "Can anything good come out of Nazareth?" Bob Marley comes from one of the poorest regions in Jamaica. The village in Qunu where Nelson Mandela was born is not that great. Malcolm X grew up on the streets. Do not be shaken by the shack. You were born there for a reason. You were born there so you may observe what is unfolding there and learn from it as you go out and try to change the world.'

When I tried to talk to him about the things we were taught by people like Mrs Bopape – stating that I would prefer to be taught about how King Shaka defeated the British than about the concentration camps in Germany, about how Sekhukhune and Nghunghunyane led the troops from the north – and when I asked him why we were still being taught about the French Revolution and not about Paul Kruger, the man I had seen in town, he would simply say, 'I understand where you are coming from. Look at the Anglo-Boer War, for instance.'

I would quickly jump in. 'What is that?'

'It was two nations fighting about who should take our land. To put it in terms you will understand, it is two guys popping into your house and starting to fight about who should take it,' he would patiently explain.

The conversations I had with Mr Mathibela developed my conscience. It is for the same reason that, today, I fully support efforts to decolonise school and university curriculums. Because doing so will help people of colour out of the poverty that we find ourselves in today. An identity crisis coupled with ignorance will worsen our problems.

I had noticed that even our educators did not bring their children to our schools. Even my hero, Mr Mathibela, wouldn't take his daughter to a government school. Instead, he took her to a Model C school.

This made me realise something: if you were a shop owner and you did not use your own products, but went out to buy similar products from a different shop, you were simply acknowledging the faults with your shop or its products.

Chapter 15

Saulridge: Mr President

In 2012, I finally reached matric and changed uniform, just as my sisters had done before me. I no longer wore grey flannel trousers and a maroon-and-white tie. Instead, I wore navy-blue trousers, a white buttoned shirt and the same tie my sisters had worn. In fact, Akani had given me her tie. Those who could afford to buy the maroon school blazer were advised to do so. A new cardigan jersey was introduced for the matriculants to replace the maroon-and-white machine-knitted jersey.

Our school was very crowded. On average, there were forty learners in a class. In March, after waiting through a long process, we got four mobile classrooms, which were containers. The mobile classes were very hot – they were more like shacks. But we didn't care, because they really set us apart from the other learners. Our science class was room 26. They placed us very close to the administration building – next to Mr Mangena's office to be more precise. This meant we had a different uniform and brand-new single desks, and we were treated differently from the other learners.

Our class was star-studded. We had every cool kid in our class, from rappers to dancers to pastors. We even had a soccer player who was playing for Orlando Pirates' development side. Senzo Sethole was his name. Nelson Ndhima was also a promising player. He used to play for good teams in town.

I was extremely popular among our peers and educators. Subsequently, I was elected as the boy class rep by my peers, and Precious Modiba was elected as the girl class rep.

Mr Mangena believed in us. Even though he never taught me any subjects, he made me feel like I could do it. He would frequently single me out at assembly in front of over a thousand learners: 'Clinton Chauke and Precious Modiba, by the end of this year I want to see you shaking the hand of the minister of education, Angie Motshekga.' He said this statement on the first day of school. 'The General' as we nicknamed him, believed in all of us. Like Mr Mathibela, Mr Mangena not only gave us education, but hope. Sometimes, we did not need much – just knowing that someone believed in us was enough. Seeing Mr Mangena's compassion made me realise that being a good person was hard – it involves being a good teacher, a good brother, a good son, a good father, a good uncle, a good spouse, a good citizen. These things are not easy. At Saulridge, I learnt that my greatness was inside me.

Because of pressure from Mr Mangena, I spent most of my time in the library. I was forced to study in the library, because at home I didn't have a desk and it was always noisy. There was a tavern just across from our shack, so the conditions were always bad. I realised that the library silently contained the books that contained hidden truths.

I had also cut off watching too much television. There was a good reason, I thought, why they called programmes 'programmes' – because they programmed my mind. A lot of times, they told us that to achieve our dreams we had to be thin or light-skinned or tall. And I saw a lot of young people working very hard to alter themselves to conform to those standards. What I thought people lacked the most was patience. They just wanted things to happen overnight, like in those TV shows I used to watch with Akani. I chose to follow my own programme and rejected being programmed. I refused to be told that I could achieve my dreams overnight or that there was some sort of shortcut to success without pain or hard work. It also pained my heart to see young people imitating the rappers, smoking weed and not caring about life. What made me angrier was that, when there were events, I would see those rappers on the red carpet looking fresh, dressed all nicely and posing with their families. The limelight was fake! I cut out watching TV to focus on my books.

I would study in the community library or cross-night at school. I remember, once, I was cross-nighting at school with my friends. At about 10 p.m., we went out to buy *sphatlo/kota* (a quarter of a loaf of bread with potato chips). We had a conversation with the *kota* guy while he prepared the chips. He seemed sceptical, unimpressed by our efforts to do well at school. I got it: when your dreams have been dashed over and over again, it is best to stop hoping. I understood where he was coming from. Seeing your dreams not materialise can make you lower your expectations. I, too, had been taught to panic, because I had seen a lot with my own eyes. But I did not want to give in to fear. So, I told him that one day I would drive a BMW 5 Series.

'Keep dreaming. We have all been there, boy, but look at me today – stuck here selling *kota*,' he shot back.

What he said challenged me. But it also killed my hopes. From that time, I did not like to talk about my expectations because I was afraid they might not be met. Each of us has our own deeply held beliefs that we are not ready to share with anyone. We would rather let people see them as they unfold. But, during that time, I would still ask myself the few simple questions that every youth asks. Am I going to drive my dream car? Am I going to live in my dream house?

My father always told me that *ku humelela ka wena ku sukela eku titshembheni ka wena* (confidence is an ingredient of a man's success). I always oozed confidence – well, it was arrogance, in fact. I felt like I owned the world. I thought that anything that happened without me at school sucked. I even ran for the Representative Council of Learners (RCL) with the same attitude, for I was Clinton and I was destined to be president, as my father had had a vision. I had the right qualifications to run to be on the RCL since I was a class rep and Jerry Siwelo had trained me in public speaking.

I remember the day I went to assembly to campaign to be on the RCL against fifty-five other learners. I was

146

very happy and jolly that day. Part of my joy was because I was wearing the school blazer that my friend had lent me. Of course, I could not afford a blazer. 'The school blazer is a luxury. As long as you have a shirt and trousers, that is enough,' my mother reassured me. My mother had a way of making me feel proud of being poor. Even though our home was a shack, I never felt ashamed at home. My mother was the guiding force behind us. Every day, she would remind us, '*Hambi sweswi mi tshamaku amazingini, tsundzukani leswaku ami mazingi nwina* (Even though you may be living in the shack, know that you are not the shack you are living in).' I had learnt earlier that, whether you lived in a mansion or a shack, an RDP house or a traditional four-room house, whether you were from a suburb or a township or a village, there was no better feeling than being at home. Home was not a building for me, but the people and the feeling.

Anyway, the blazer gave me confidence. I do not remember much about the speech I gave that day. I only remember one line, at which the whole school erupted in laughter: 'And there at the feeding scheme, I don't promise you KFC.' All I could hear, everywhere I went that Friday morning, was, 'Hey Mr KFC.' I knew at that moment that my name would be on the successful candidates list come Monday.

On Monday, Mr KFC was elected deputy president of the RCL. I came to learn why politicians love to use catchphrases. I learnt that 'Yes we can', or 'I have a dream', or 'I am an African' were not just silly words – they had the power to move people.

Precious Modiba won the presidency. Peter Maluleke was our secretary, and Wisani 'Maseven' Chauke was his deputy. Sfiso 'Dimera' Mazibuko was our sports officer. Letlhogonolo Mola was our treasurer and Millicent Phala was her deputy. Kagiso Mothapo was our arts and culture officer. Lets Sehata was our education officer. We went to Rosina Sedibane School in Laudium, where we were inducted.

Precious Modiba had a thin body, so those kids used to call *me* Mr President. They thought I was running the show. In truth, Precious is the one who was calling most of the shots. I had a good working relationship with Precious, but we were clearly not friends. She was friends with my best friend Success and our maths teacher, Nokuthula Khumalo.

Being in the RCL really helped me to stay focused on my books. It even changed my perception of being cool. I started to take myself a little bit more seriously, because some kids looked up to me. I disciplined myself in two activities: reading and writing. I started to write poems about life in the squatter camp. A lot of people did not like to visit the squatter camps, so I felt that my pen was the only instrument that could take them there. Some learners were uncomfortable when we preached this message; some were completely silent. Being quiet was not always a sign of wisdom to me. Some people kept quiet and shied away from engaging with serious issues. In the process, they became complete idiots. I knew this for sure because I was once in a taxi and two ladies I knew were arguing. Even though I knew who was right, I chose not to interfere, so I kept quiet. I later met the lady who I honestly thought was right. I told her that I thought she had been right.

'Why didn't you say it on the spot, then?' she asked. 'I am sure you are going to say the same thing to Mavis,' she concluded. Although I had honestly thought she was right, I appeared to be not credible enough because I had not stood up when it mattered the most.

On the RCL, we were entrusted to enforce discipline among our peers. One of the things that I always struggled with was stopping the graffiti on the walls. You know those 'Clinton was here in 1994' marks? I recalled what Mr Mangena always said at assembly, that Bob Mabena, the legendary radio DJ, used to go to our school. So, one day, I gave myself the task of looking for Bob's graffiti somewhere on the walls. To my surprise, I could not find it. This made me realise that you do not become legendary through what you claim to be – what you do distinguishes you. I realised that I could go to all the public places I had been in and write that I had been there – but if I did not do something meaningful, I would probably be forgotten. Greatness was never a given in my eyes. It was to be earned. If my presence was noticed, then my absence would be too.

I still remember the joy of wearing a school uniform. Doing so freed us from the need to compete for recognition among our peers. Precious Modiba wore her school uniform with pride. I was so inspired by her that I did the same. When a school uniform is worn with pride, it instils a new positive attitude in an entire learner community. We formed a good team. We would stand at the school gate in Moroe Street and monitor latecomers, usually taking them to Mr Mangena's office for disciplinary procedures.

Mr Poo would sometimes join us and deal with girls who wore miniskirts. Girls were required to wear longer skirts with a white blouse. If they failed to do so, Mr Poo would deal with them accordingly. For all his efforts, Mr Poo was dedicated to disciplining the learners and we respected him for that. Female teachers like Mam Mmupe and Mam Kekana would often come and assist with girls who wore weaves. Some girls wore expensive weaves and the female teachers were not impressed. They would ask them to cut them off, or they would remove them themselves using a pair of scissors. At times, I felt like it was jealousy!

In winter, we allowed our fellow learners to wear school jumpers under their blazers, but only when we said they could. Otherwise they'd have to take their jumpers off!

Casual clothes were worn when we decided. We usually suggested the occasion on Fridays. We called it 'mufti' and pupils were required to pay R5. You would find learners in all kinds of clothes, but you could easily see which learners came from well-established families and who came from poor families.

Being in the RCL was fun, especially during events. I remember, once, during the athletics event for which all the high schools gathered at Lucas Moripe Stadium, we printed the tickets and sold them for our own benefit. That's how we repaid ourselves for being in the forum.

We also did the same for the talent show and the Mr and Ms Saulridge pageant, since we were the organisers. Before I was in the RCL, I had attended the pageant only once. Because, even though I was cool, I was also a Mzalwane (Christian). So, the bashes in Saulsville Arena were not really an ideal place for me; once the learners got drunk, they would start to fight with the teachers, so I always boycotted them.

We were required to attend the SGB (school governing body) meetings. There was a lady who would usually come with baked cookies and serve us as the meeting progressed. SGB meetings were my favourite meetings because of the cookies.

At our school, we did have a little computer lab, but we were never allowed to use the computers. By the time I was in the RCL, we fought hard until they allowed us to use them. I remember the first day they allowed us in. Our teacher only taught us to open a Gmail account. He helped the whole class to create their e-mail accounts and that was it. It was funny how they only allowed us to open e-mails as if our inboxes had something important in them. But personally, I am grateful for the chance to have opened an e-mail account – it is the e-mail address I am still using to this day.

We proposed the provision of buses, because our learners – including me – had to walk great distances to school. The City of Tshwane heard our cry and provided us with buses that would transport learners from different sections in Mshongo, Selbourne Side and Lotus Gardens. The buses would fetch them in the morning from key stopping points and drop them off again after school.

We also requested a school pavement and the replacement of the barbed-wire fence with palisade fencing, which we got! And, because of our constant presence at the school gate, latecoming dropped as well.

In the end, being in the RCL made me cocky. I started to lose my cool and became a bit disrespectful to my teachers. One teacher who never bought into my nonsense was Mrs Bopape, who taught Life Sciences. I remember once I was sitting with Success and we were paging through a section that explained Down Syndrome. Success scrawled funny marks on the picture of kids who displayed the symptoms. Upon seeing me laughing, Mrs Bopape thought I was laughing at the kids. She yelled, '*Chauke awu betere wena* (Mr Chauke, don't assume you are better than them).' Then she added, 'Just because you are on the RCL doesn't mean you are special.'

Chapter 16

Saulridge: Final year

Our struggle to pick up girls continued throughout our high school years. But being in the RCL opened a lot of doors for me, including the girls. They would throw themselves at me. But I was a typical Mzalwane – I was indestructible. I never kissed a girl until I got to matric.

One day, as I was walking to class from the administration office, I met three girls. They were in Grade 10 and were really barbaric. They asked if they could have a kiss with me since it was international kiss day. I didn't even know that there was such a day. I accepted the offer. My first kiss was rather shorter than I anticipated. I reached out with my mouth open. That is how I saw people kissing on *Generations* when I watched with Akani. The girl simply never opened her mouth. I was embarrassed. She gave me a kiss you would give to a toddler. By the third girl, I had perfected the art but unfortunately she had bad breath, so I stopped halfway. She was clearly still enjoying the kiss from Mr President. Maybe she thought she had a chance, poor girl! By the time I got to class, I clicked that I had got three kisses from three different girls. That was too many kisses in one day for a man who had never kissed a girl.

But the state of not having a girl really started to get on my nerves. Some of the kids started to disrespect me, saying, '*Gwa tswana awu joli mus* (You don't even date).' But 'Don't date, you are still in high school' was preached at church, and my shyness around girls was very real. Seeing all this, Success and I decided to form an organisation known as Tinghwenda, the Xitsonga term for 'bachelors'. The name came from our vernacular class. Our teacher, Mr Mashele, once asked us, '*Wanuna wo pfumala nsati i yini?* (What do you call a man who is unmarried?)'. No one in the class knew the answer. After a while, he gave it to us in Xitsonga: '*I nghwendha* (It's bachelor).' The whole class erupted into laughter. My classmates really struggled with Xitsonga. There was one group at the back, consisting of Rhulani, Calvin and Glen. They didn't take the class seriously. When they heard a weird Xitsonga name, they would simply laugh, as if they were not Vatsonga themselves. Rhulani was one of those show-offs, a bragging, self-satisfied township boy. He was the type who would never have been associated with Limpopo. Rhulani was so embarrassed by Limpopo – in the same way as some African Americans are embarrassed by Africa despite their being, in Bob Marley's words, 'Buffalo Soldiers', who fought for America.

After forming Tinghwenda, we made it look like it was the best thing to be single – to the point where the guys who had girlfriends thought they were missing out. We started to recruit people who were too shy to approach girls, or those who had difficulty relating to the girls. Sylvester Ndou, for example, was struggling. The problem for him was that he was too soft. He was once dumped by a girl who told him this; he was committed to our organisation from that point. Erens Mathole used to date fat girls and we dissed him for it; he joined the organisation as a result. Kabelo Manyaka was a very quiet and shy gym guy; he found refuge in our organisation. Livewell Chauke was not gentle with girls. He had a record of once slapping a girl. Plus, he never had time for them; the organisation was a good place for him. Success was book-smart, so he couldn't relate to girls; hence, he was a co-founder. I mobilised all these guys. I would give them free tickets when we had events at school since I was on the RCL.

Tinghwenda was a self-sufficient machine. We would save money and go to the movies at Sterland Ster-Kinekor in Arcadia, with no girls around. I remember we went to watch *The Hunger Games* in 2012. Vukosi Mathe and Joshua Shimbambu, who were fairly good with women, admired us greatly.

But our organisation had its critics as well. Guys like Katlego Ngobeni never bought into our madness. He would often come to our group and say, '*Yoo i* boys choir *ka hiso!* (It's a boys' choir in here!)' I would explain the situation and he would respond, '*No buti, mi chava vanhonyani nwina, ahi vhayi hala ntaku kumela one* plus *u* president (No, my brother, you guys are afraid to approach girls. Let's go this side, I will hook you with one. Plus, you are the president). Katlego was very good with girls. Since Masizane, everybody had known that he was a ladies' man.

During breaktime, which lasted for about forty-five minutes, we resumed eating at the feeding scheme. We now had the knowledge that the feeding scheme aimed to foster better-quality education by enhancing our active learning capacity. We made it look cool again. We would buy atchar from the hawkers who came to sell at our school, and spice up our food.

There were different types of people we would see during lunch breaks. Some bought from the hawkers. Others bought at the tuck shop. We had those who ate from the feeding scheme. Then we had some who had pride: they didn't have money, but their pride wouldn't take them to the feeding scheme. We had the young thugs, who would be gambling in the toilets. Some responsible boys would play soccer on a small roadway close to the main gate. And, we had Bazalwane (the born-again Christians). They ate the word of God. They would usually meet to discuss the Bible under the tree next to Mr Mangena's office. I was a two-faced Mzalwane: at school, people didn't know that I was a churchgoer.

Finally, there was one distinctively snobbish group consisting of Melvin Khumalo, Brian Baloyi, and Glen, Oscar and Shane Setsweni. They would usually go out and buy plates of food at the market at Saulsville station. They never associated themselves with the other learners. They would only talk to me because I was on the RCL.

By 11:45 a.m., when the train came back from Saulsville, we knew that breaktime was over.

At the end of the year, we never had a matric dance, what they call a prom in America. It is a day designed to bid farewell to the school's senior students. Although we acted as if we were disappointed, the news was great for the Tinghwenda nation: if we went to a matric dance, we would need a date, which would clash with our organisation's core values. Mam Mmupe is the one who sabotaged our matric dance. It was the first time since I had been going to Saulridge that they didn't have a matric dance. The guys always teased me for this misfortune: 'They cancelled the matric dance because the president doesn't have a date.' (Mam Mmupe, the Accounting teacher, had organised the event through the years. Her Accounting class that year had disrespected her, and reported her to the principal for not arriving to teach her class regularly. This made her so mad that she decided not to organise a matric dance at all.)

By this time, I really wanted a girlfriend. The treasurer of the RCL, Letlhogonolo – who was also crowned Miss Saulridge – always gave good signs that she wanted us to date, and we did, indeed, have good chemistry. And since the guys played around by suggesting that I was the one to blame for the matric dance, Letlhogonolo also said, '*Ba cancetsi* matric dance *ka gore aona* girlfriend (They have cancelled the matric dance because you don't have a girlfriend).' But my shyness and what I was hearing at church made me pass up the chance with Letlhogonolo. She was very cute, a Mona Lisa type of girl. She had these long, natural dreadlocks. Her appearance seemed simple to emulate, yet it would be impossible for anyone to do so. She was a true African princess. Her humility and beauty were disturbing, and always made me fantasise about things that are simply unprintable. During our RCL meetings after school, we would always flirt. Afterwards, I would escort her to the Saulsville station, since she stayed in Sunnyside in town.

But, back to class. English and Vernacular were the subjects I liked the most. Mr Mashele always gave us advice about the importance of holding on to our roots. He always reminded us to visit home during the holidays. By home, he meant Limpopo. He was against the idea of us claiming that Atteridgeville was our home. He hated all the ills of the urban areas, and failed to hide it. (I now know why Mr Mashele was angry. He was crying for the broken tribes, the broken customs, the broken traditions. He was crying for the broken people. He was crying for the people like Rhulani.)

The only thing that connected me to my roots was the type of music that we listened to at home. We listened to traditional Xitsonga music. In fact, we only listened to Thomas Chauke Na Shinyori Sisters in my household. My mother was very strict about what we listened to and watched. Her favourite was a little song called 'Xipereta'. It was a song about a woman who was married to a lazy man. The Shinyori Sisters sang about how this lady was doing all she could to survive with her children. The song was really applicable to my father. He hated Thomas's songs because they would expose him. '*Tina swicele tinghoma leti* (These songs are divisive),' he would say.

My father listened to Zozo, a popular Tshivenḓa musician. That is how I learnt to speak Tshivenḓa – through my father's music. He said it reminded him of Venḓa before they were removed from there in the late sixties: '*Tintsundzuxa Venḓa he vafana* (These songs remind me of Venḓa, my boy),' he would say. I knew he was lying because when they moved from Venḓa he was only six years old. My father was good at lying. But let me not say that my father was a liar – my mother wouldn't like it. Let's just say my father was a highly creative man.

In 2011, we saw the introduction of a flamboyant Xitsonga artist, Benny Baloyi, who used the stage name of Benny Mayengani. Mayengani was a very controversial Xitsonga musician whose lyrics incited vulgarity and were very boastful. He made the Vatsonga, who were known to be respectful and dignified, very uncomfortable. He referenced Jesus in his songs and won himself a cult-like following – in fact, he copied Jesus, referring to his supporters as *valandzeri* (followers). I fell in love with his music. It reminded me of my early days back in Bevhula. But, deep down, I knew that had I stayed in Bevhula my whole life, I probably would have wound up being a wayward and illiterate young man.

Mayengani was very talented, and had a golden voice. His remarkable talent aside, there is one thing I liked about him: he was very confident. He had incredible charisma, a trait that draws people to you like bees to nectar. He was contrary to everything that was represented in the Shangaan image. Mayengani was proud of our language. When he stood up to perform, it was like

159

he took all the years of oppression and ridicule from black society, absorbed it in his voice, then sang out very proudly and beautifully. And, even though he was swearing, kicking ass and taking names, he was our shining star. He made me proud to be Shangaan.

A few years later, I saw the same pride when Sho Madjozi rose and shot straight to stardom. Unlike Mayengani, Madjozi didn't sing traditional music – she went straight to hip-hop. And since hip-hop is all about standing up to the 'man', Madjozi entered that field proudly wearing her *xibelani* (traditional Xitsonga skirt) and rapping in Xitsonga. Sho Madjozi and Mayengani were our two cool kids.

There was one song I liked best from Mayengani's albums, called '*Misava yima ni chika*'. The song basically spoke about a man who had married the wrong woman after being dumped by his first lover. In it, Mayengani sang about how he wished time could stop so he could go back and start all over again. Mayengani was Benny Baloyi's alter ego. He became my alter ego, too. He said things that I felt were true but couldn't say, because I was afraid of society.

At school, I was very good at Xitsonga because I had lived in the village and remained rooted in the culture at home. I had an advantage over the other guys in our class, who had lived in Atteridgeville all their lives. Katlego Ngobeni was good at Physical Science. My best friend Success Nobela was good at Mathematics. In fact, he was a maths genius. We used to call him Prof. We also had Charmaine and Charlotte, who were impressive. Collins Maluleke also joined in. Precious Modiba was excellent in all her subjects. All seven of us, we were always competing.

I enjoyed English class more, though, especially when we would read stories. Reading was a challenge for most of my classmates. They were shy to read aloud, even though they were in the highest grade at school. Precious Modiba was the one who would always volunteer to read, because she had prepared at home. I would do the same thing in Xitsonga class.

My English teacher, Refiloe Bodibe, was a darling. I remember that she would give us books to go and read. The following day, she would ask whether we had understood them. Every time, we would go back to class with an idea of what we were going to say. One Friday morning, she gave us *Macbeth*. When she asked for our reviews the following Monday, the whole class was dead silent – including Precious. *Macbeth* was a very difficult book. The English that was used in that book was very difficult. It was painful because our future was going to be decided according to how well we understood that book. Mrs Bodibe tried by all means to explain it to us. As Precious would read, we would miss the jokes and punchlines. Mrs Bodibe would frequently stop Precious and ask us, 'Didn't you hear that was a joke?' I would immediately laugh out loud, pretending I had got the joke.

Not only *Macbeth*, but other books such as *The Merchant of Venice* and *Romeo and Juliet* were very hard for us to process. There is also a short story called 'The

Secret Life of Walter Mitty'. To this day, I do not understand what was happening in that story.

Our school never prescribed African literature. There was nothing that spoke of Africa or the people who looked like us in the books that we read. In deliberately doing so – omitting to teach us about ourselves – the school was teaching us to hate our heritage. When we read *Animal Farm*, Mrs Bodibe would compare the then ANC Youth League leader Julius Malema to Snowball and President Zuma to Napoleon.

Mathematics was one subject I did not like, because it never allowed room for argument or debate. If the answer was four, it stood that way, no argument. Our Mathematics teacher, Nokuthula Khumalo, was Zimbabwean. Whenever she wanted us to relate to a particular concept, she would speak in Sepedi. Since she was not that good at the language, we laughed at her when she pronounced a word incorrectly. What really struck me was that she never laughed at us when we did not know how to work out a Maths problem. Instead, she helped us. That is what I tried to do in those days: instead of laughing at people, I tried to help them.

As the year slipped past, Mr Mathibela would help us with our application forms for further study. While I was filling in the application forms from the University of Pretoria (UP) and Tshwane University of Technology (TUT), I realised that the admission requirements were fifty per cent, but the pass mark in our school was thirty per cent. If you did not play to score, then I did not see the point of playing at all. I could not justify this, and believed that I was the victim of a broken system. I then thought to myself: since research plays a crucial role in innovation, invention and discovery, what kind of researchers were we producing with a pass mark of thirty per cent? With an education system that did not even attempt to address the problems that were facing the country, the ministry of education aimed to conquer the future. But how could they have fixed the system using the same tactics that had created the problem? It was like killing a cow that you wanted to milk – it did not make sense to me. While I was filling in the forms, I made a vow to Mr Mathibela that I would study mining, since he had stated there was a lot of money in it; Mr Mathibela loved me, and I also loved him.

By the time the trial exams approached, a gentleman offered to help us with Physical Science. While it should not matter, the gentleman was white. His name was Jonathan Smith. He was a lecturer at Tshwane South College in Atteridgeville. Mr Smith would go to the Model C schools and look at their syllabus. The textbooks they used were different from ours. Why did we use different textbooks if we were going to write the same exam? For example, the Physical Science textbook we used would spend half a chapter explaining how and where Newton was seated when the apple fell. We did not know whether we would be examined on that history, and our teacher was not that good, and could not tell us whether or not we needed to study the history. As a result, we would study the wrong stuff. In the Model C schools, however, you would find textbooks with one paragraph explaining the history and the rest being content – explaining the laws of gravitation and formulas. The teachers were highly skilled, and would guide the learners through what to focus on for the exam. On average, their pass rate was always above ninety per cent. From that point on, the future was bright for those learners.

The implication was that the wealthy people would continue to thrive, while the poor people would continue to lag.

Today, I wonder what Mr Smith's agenda was, though. In my experience, a white person will never help you without expecting something in return. I think I'm being racist now, but I'm just being like white people: I have never met a white person who is not racist (either consciously or unconsciously). I'm probably getting myself into trouble now . . . but I'm just kidding, white people. You guys are good people. Let's just play along; it's better that way. More chains, if you know what I mean. We have been sweet-talking the white man since the day he first set foot in the Mother City. (I wonder whose mother it is, though?) We are still sweet-talking him: we can't tell him how we really feel about him.

Still, in the end, Katlego managed to get two distinctions, in Maths and Physical Science. Success got ninety-one per cent for Maths. Precious got seven distinctions. She made headlines in a local newspaper called the *Tshwane Sun*: 'Precious Modiba, Atteridgeville's top dog'.

My sister Tsakani registered for online notification of my results. She recited my results before I had seen them. I didn't really believe them. I then bought a newspaper called the *Sowetan*. I looked for my name. There were no brackets next to my name. I was happy for Precious, but my heart was broken because I didn't get any distinctions – not even for my strongest subject, home language. I always gave the excuse that Precious and Katlego had only succeeded because they did not stay in a shack. They stayed in the proper houses of the township and they had strict parents who always monitored their progress at school. I may have been very bitter, but I had a point: after school, I would have to go and get water from the JoJo tank in our squatter camp. Obviously, I couldn't compare to students who did not have to use a candle to study. But my argument was shaky: Success also stayed in a shack. His home was not very far from mine.

I managed to get five Cs and two Bs. I got 61 per cent for Mathematics, 65 per cent for Physical Science, 67 per cent for Life Science, 68 per cent for Geography and English, 71 per cent for Life Orientation and 74 per cent for Xitsonga. What was even sadder for me was that the following year I was forced to take a gap year. This was due to a mistake I had made of not applying for university on time.

Success, the twins and Collins went to TUT, Joshua went to the University of Johannesburg (UJ), Katlego marched to Wits, Precious went to UP, and I went straight to depression land . . .

Chapter 17

Gap year

Unlike the kids in the Western world who voluntarily take a gap year after high school, I was forced to take one. This didn't help me, because the situation in my home was very bad for me to be losing a year. Our teachers at Saulridge always advised us to apply early for university admission. I was paying the price for not listening.

I always wanted to go to Wits or UP, top universities in the country. But, looking at my marks, they wouldn't allow me to study anything serious like actuarial science or chartered accountancy or engineering. My marks would get me into a top university in South Africa, like the University of Cape Town (UCT) or Wits or UP, but I could only study to become a teacher or nurse or social worker there. I didn't want to study for a low-paying job that the system had designed mostly for black people.

I took my chances and applied for mining engineering at Wits, civil engineering at UP, electrical engineering at TUT and mining engineering at UJ. My sister Tsakani is the one who gave me money to apply – another of her black tax instalments.

After applying for admission to these four institutions,

I sat at home. My mother advised me to apply for a learner's licence. Akani's friend Dorcas Mashaba gave me her past question papers. I still remember that day. I went to Centurion with my brother-in-law Saddam, Neo Shilaluke and Bro Phyllis. All of us passed, except for Bro Phyllis. It was very awkward when we came home in the taxi – we couldn't laugh at Bro Phyllis since he was a very humble guy. We didn't have a car at home, so I had no clue how to drive. I couldn't go for lessons at the driving school, because we didn't have money. So, my learner's licence ended up expiring.

I would just chill at home. Every day, I woke up to watch men and women grappling with the challenges that faced the vast majority of people in our beloved country.

I saw a young boy who grew up without a father figure in the house, looked around him, and saw nothing but things that discouraged him. I watched him finally decide that taking drugs would be the ultimate solution. I have seen what drugs such as *nyaope* have done to our brothers and some of our sisters: in the words of President Mbeki, they have lost their sanity because 'to be sane is to invite pain'.

I saw a young girl who grew up without a mother, being vulnerable and finally realising that maybe that old uncle who promised her an escape from poverty, promised her heaven and earth, maybe he was not so bad after all. I watched him as he tricked her and impregnated her and left her as a teen mom.

I saw a young man who had the grades, the drive and

the will, but was burdened with the responsibility of raising his three siblings. I watched him drop out of school and go out to look for a job to make ends meet.

I saw a young and beautiful lady who had many boyfriends. I watched her as different cars came to pick her up to go out partying. I sat there wondering what exactly she was celebrating.

I saw a father who went home drunk every night, but never had money to pay school fees or buy something for his children's lunchboxes. I watched him and wondered what made him drink.

I saw a single mother who worked very hard. I watched her sitting on her bed late at night wondering how she would be able to pay tuition fees for her A-student child.

Occasionally, I would see my neighbour getting up very early in the morning to catch the first train to work. I watched him getting robbed and finally coming to the conclusion that he should quit his job because his life was in danger.

I think all these statements could easily have been true about me, too. The only difference between me and these people is that I had a remarkable mother who was determined to see me succeed, and I responded to her efforts.

After observing all these people, I would wonder whether I was living in the bush, looking at the infrastructure around me – or the lack of it. Occasionally, when it rained, I would make sure that I was at home so I could shift some of our stuff because of the leaking roof. During winter, I would watch them as load shedding took their electricity. When I took a stroll around the place, I noticed that our area was filthy. Giant rats ate the food and destroyed the furniture. There was rubbish everywhere. There were fires in our area, caused mostly by illegal electrical connections. There was a big problem with *izinyoka* (cable thieves). Our pit toilet got full, so my father dug another hole just next to the previous one. The ground near our shack caved in. The huge hole kept on getting bigger! We slept outside, afraid that our shack would cave in with us inside.

I am not trying to paint myself as a typical African child, as the Western world had made us out to be. The squatter camp was my reality and I had to normalise its poverty. There were times when I looked at places like Sandton, Fourways and Hatfield and had to wonder whether I shared citizenship with the people who stayed in those places. It was as if I was trapped on a lonely island of poverty in the midst of vast material prosperity. Everywhere I looked, I saw crushed dreams. I learnt that I had been raised in the squatter camps of Atteridgeville – the real part of Atteridgeville.

I am not the only one who saw the ills of my community. Other residents were fed up with these poor conditions. Alarming calls were made about poor service delivery to our ward councillor, Makopa Makola. One of the community members even went as far as saying that perhaps trashing the streets and burning tyres was the only remaining option, as no other attempts had yielded any results. Protesters gathered along Maunde Street one Wednesday morning with plans to burn tyres and block the main road. The protests started, with burning tyres and placards calling for an end to deprivation.

Makola said a memorandum had been accepted by a City of Tshwane representative, but the residents didn't believe him. '*Ba nagana nkare rea gafa* (They think we are stupid),' said an angry squatter. The mayor of Tshwane – Kgosientso Ramokgopa, who was born in Atteridgeville – said they wanted to make Pretoria a world-class city, but how could they achieve that when we were living like animals?

Residents saw it as a disgrace to live the way we did, while those in mansions in the city lived like kings.

The municipality had clearly not grasped the suffering we endured. Some pregnant women lost their babies. Others gave birth in their shacks because they would have had to be pushed down the steep, rock-littered roads in a wheelbarrow to get to the ambulance in Maunde Street. '*Ke gale re lwa, from letsatsi la mathomo re fithla mo, mothlomongwe if* president *ye ka tla batle re utlwa* (We have been fighting since day one. Maybe if the president came to visit us and see how we suffer, we would get services),' another squatter said.

During the winter, Mshongo was full of all kinds of murders. I recall, one Friday morning walking to school with my sisters, finding a body of an unknown man lying on the ground. It was routine – another person's life, squashed like an insect. He'd been shot but not robbed. His cellphone was still in his pocket. The police gave the residents a chance to view the body, but no one recognised him. Captain Thomas Mufamadi of the Atteridgeville police would sometimes give briefings on the crime scenes. It was during this time that my cousin, Gabriel Baloyi – who stayed not far from us – was shot five times in the early morning on his way to work. He survived by a miracle, but uses a wheelchair to this day. It was out of this frustration that the people would resort to mob justice when they found a culprit. They would simply shout, '*Vimba!* (Arrest!)' Within a few minutes, the robber would be on the ground with blood streaming out of his body.

Cars couldn't even drive on our roads. There was no light in the early mornings when we walked to school. We were sometimes robbed. Some people were raped on the mountain towards Laudium in the east. Without a doubt, the silence of the government was too loud! And it was all written off to incompetence and/or corruption.

In August, all my application results were communicated to me. I'd been rejected at Wits. I'd been rejected at UP, the university where my mother was a cleaner. I'd been accepted at UJ to study for a diploma in mining engineering. UJ was ranked tenth out of the twenty-three universities in the country. My mediocre matric results saw me studying at a mediocre university. I was angry: I wanted to follow my friends to Wits or UP, but the system had rejected me.

By late September, I was tutoring three learners and refreshing my own memory in preparation for the unknown of university life.

Chapter 18

UJ: Robin Crest

After waiting for a full year, I finally moved to Johannesburg to start my first year at UJ. I arrived at Robin Crest male residence, my new home.

My brothers from His Rest church, Dennis Williams and Neo Shilaluke, together with my parents, escorted me to Robin Crest. We arrived at the parking lot very early in the morning and two Vatsonga security guards welcomed us as if we were at home.

'*Se mi huma kwihi kaya papa?* (Where are you from?)' one of the guards asked my father.

'*Hi huma ka-Bevhula mara hi tshama hala Atteridgeville* (We are from Bevhula village, but we are currently staying in Atteridgeville),' my father replied. After a small chat, the security guards led us to the residence manager's office, which was on the second floor of the eleven-floor residence.

'*Siyani amukela bazali* (We welcome you, our dear parents),' she began. She then gave us the keys and we moved to the fifth floor. My suitcases were heavy. Dennis and Neo quickly helped me get my luggage to my apartment, number 506. The apartment was two double rooms for first-year students, one single room for a senior student, a kitchen, and a bathroom with a shower. This was a very good environment to study and do well in, unlike the shack I called home back in Atteridgeville.

Inside my room, I found my roommate, who had already moved in. Lubabalo Mdoda was his name. He came from the mining town of Westonaria in Johannesburg. His father was a miner. This was the man I was going to spend the year with. After greeting Lubabalo and chatting for a while, my parents, Dennis and Neo didn't stay much longer. I remember I wanted to cry when they left me there. I was worried about the prospect of being alone; I felt isolated. But I was one of the many students who were packing and unpacking their belongings that day.

After unpacking, we were called for a meeting by the residence manager. We took a lift from the fifth floor down to the first. We passed the laundry room on the right and the TV room on the left and walked into the study, where the meeting was going to be held. She welcomed us. Somewhere among her closing remarks, she started to give us warnings about the city. 'Walk with other people whenever you can. Let a friend or roommate know where you are going,' she said. 'Keep your bag closed, and hold on to it at all times when you are out. If you need directions, look for someone in uniform – preferably a policeman – and ask for help,' she added.

Robin Crest had an Engen garage to the left and the infamous and iconic Ponte City to the right. Ponte City, or the Vodacom building, was a skyscraper in the Berea neighbourhood, just next to the suburb of Hillbrow. The fifty-five-storey cylindrical apartment block made all the flats around our campus look very tiny. It is the tallest residential skyscraper in Africa. Behind it was a huge, open field where the criminal gangs lived. In front of us were three school residences (Sivebeek, South Point and Habitat) and the Johannesburg stadium. Rea Vaya buses passed in front of our residence via Saratoga Avenue.

Our residence was very close to the Doornfontein campus, where I was going to study. UJ had four campuses. It came into existence as the result of a merger between the Rand Afrikaans University (RAU), the Technikon Witwatersrand (TWR) and Vista University. The Bunting Road and Doornfontein campuses used to be Technikon Witwatersrand. Our campus was the ugliest of the four campuses. It was very different from what I had seen on pamphlets and brochures when I was applying. The Soweto campus used to be Vista University. The then United States president Barack Obama had visited a year prior to my enrolment. The Auckland Park campus was the most popular and most beautiful, and the main campus of the university. It was the university's centre of administration and governance. The institution used to be a whites-only institution and didn't allow black students until apartheid ended.

The street kids surrounded our campus in all directions. To the north, just over the bridge, there was China City (a shopping mall) and five school residences, including ours. To the east was Shembe church, McDonald's, Ellis Park Stadium, Johannesburg Central College, a post

174

office, I.H. Harris Primary School and the Doornfontein train station. This is where I used to take the train from when I visited home during university holidays. To the south was the Mariston Hotel, the Razzmatazz tavern, the Diplomat Hotel and the nightclub at the Royal Park Hotel, where some students would satisfy themselves with prostitutes and drugs. To the west was the stylish Saratoga Village residence, the Old Synagogue and Ponte City.

Ponte City neighboured our residence. There were illegal landlords, gangs and prostitutes there. The activities that these people engaged in had increased crime rates at the tower and in its surrounds. Many gangs moved into the back yard of our residence building, and it became extremely unsafe. I will never forget witnessing my first murder on the eve of Good Friday in 2014. I was enjoying the unrestricted and amazing view of Hillbrow when I saw gang members shooting a man. They killed that man. I saw it with my own eyes. A few minutes later, the coroner arrived. It was like I was watching a movie. But that became the normality of our lives; we would witness more murders in that back yard. Luckily for us, we never used the back entrance. We used the one in front on Saratoga Avenue, where many students from Sivebeek, South Point and Habitat, with their school bags and drawing boards, dragged themselves to the main road on their way to campus. On many occasions, students got robbed, even on the so-called safe side. When one student shouted '*Vimba!*', others would come out in numbers to deliver mob justice.

Vimba reminded me of home. When I went to university, I was very optimistic about everything. But the city of Johannesburg struck me, even though I had come from the ghetto and no ghetto was more real than Mshongo.

At night, Ponte City, with Hillbrow's other towers, formed a beautiful Johannesburg view. The German writer Norman Ohler once said that 'Ponte sums up all the hope, all the wrong ideas of modernism, all the decay, all the craziness of the city. It is a symbolic building, a sort of white whale, it is concrete fear, the tower of Babel, and yet it is strangely beautiful'. I felt very much like him when experiencing the city as an outsider. And this is what I felt like in Johannesburg – an outsider, surrounded by crime, far away from home.

But back on that first day, all the first-year students were called to the study room and given a campus tour by one of the members of the residence's leadership forum. His name was Solomon Phole, but we called him Master Single (which had something to do with his relationship status). Master Single escorted us. It was a five-minute walk. Immediately after passing the bridge, where there were a lot of beggars, we walked through the main gate of the campus. We started our tour at the student centre, which was very close to the main gate. 'This is where you are going to buy food. When you bunk classes, you will come and chill here,' Single said, as we all laughed. We then moved past the residence offices and went across to the administration building, called Maropeng. From Maropeng, we passed a beautiful lawn on our right and a huge student parking lot on our left. We then made our way to Lwazi building, which had lecture rooms and study rooms. 'When the course chows you, you will come and sleep here,' Single continued to joke with us.

We then made our way into the main lecture building, called John Orr. John Orr had seven floors. We walked upstairs; on our return, we used the lifts. We took a left and passed the toilets. Immediately after the toilets, we walked into the library. This was the place where I would later spend most of my time. We exited John Orr by passing the squash courts into a beautiful park. There were two female residences, Jeunesse and Aurum, there. Then, our little tour was over.

My only challenge at Robin Crest was the cooking part. Because I grew up surrounded by ladies, I didn't know how to cook by the time I got to res. My sister Tsakani continued her black tax payments. She is the one who would give me money to buy groceries, but I didn't know what to do with it. I had applied for a student loan through NSFAS, the National Student Financial Aid Scheme, which only covered my tuition. At UJ, NSFAS didn't give students money for food. Instead, we were given tablet computers, so we could be on par with twenty-first-century learning, we were told. I had to provide food myself. Tsakani would put off buying a new dress for herself and send me money at UJ to carry me throughout the year. My mother would often join her.

They poured everything they had into me so that I could have a better future.

Chapter 19

UJ: First year

By the time classes started in the first week of February, I was already used to Doornfontein. They were renovating the campus and extending the John Orr building to the east towards Doornfontein station, an extension that was sponsored by the Sibanye mining company. As a result of this work, we attended some classes at Ellis Park Stadium, which was very close to our school. We did this for the first few months until the extension was completed in May 2014.

The new building was named Perskor, and was connected to the John Orr building by a long bridge running over Beit Street on the eastern side of the campus. It was built mostly to accommodate engineering students.

I was studying to become a mining engineering technologist. I was preparing myself to make a living working thousands of feet underground. I was preparing myself to work in a place where all hell could suddenly break loose and I could be erased from this world in a split second. This was two years after the Marikana massacre, where the South African Police Service opened fire on a crowd of protesting mineworkers who were demanding a wage increase at the Lonmin Platinum Mine in

Marikana, North West Province. Thirty-four mineworkers were killed and more than two hundred and fifty people were arrested. The fateful event revived memories of the police brutality that people had suffered under apartheid. The massacre was the biggest incident involving police brutality since the dawn of democracy in South Africa.

I could sense my family's concerns about losing me to the profession I had chosen to pursue.

'*Mara u ta lungha nwananga?*' (My son, are you going to cope, though?)' my mother asked.

I was not sure. '*Hita vona kwele mhani* (We shall wait and see, Mom),' I replied.

Nothing forced me to study mining but my circumstances and the need for more money. I had decided to risk it all so I could give my family economic freedom. I did it because I was shack poor. Unlike most students on campus, I did not study mining because of passion – well, if it was passion, then it was passion for money. If my situation had been better, I would not have prepared myself to go and work underground where I would be constantly subjected to rockfalls. Maybe I would have pursued a career in something I *was* passionate about, like flying. I always dreamt of being a pilot. Yes, I never wanted to work on the surface of the earth, so I went underground instead. It was a matter of going big or going home. Even though I was studying the engineering skills for digging for gold, deep down I knew it was gold that I was never going to own. Today, I feel very alienated from the job I am doing: producing things I will never own.

When classes started, I was swept off my feet by one lecturer who was so full of energy. He was also the head of the Department of Mining and Mine Surveying. His name was Peter Knottenbelt. He lectured us on a module known as mining science. He was brilliant. He would always start his lectures with the words, 'You start where you start, and you end where you end.' There was one student who would usually question Mr Knottenbelt. His name was Pethedi Matshi. After Mr Knottenbelt had opened with his favourite saying, Matshi would ask, 'But sir, what do you mean?' Mr Knottenbelt would respond, 'Well, it means you start where you start and you end where you end. It explains itself.' Even though I would be in great confusion, I liked Mr Knottenbelt's saying. Matshi asked good questions and made learning more fun for us. At every class in lecture hall 106, Lwazi building, you would find him arguing with Mr Knottenbelt.

Soon after classes started, Mr Knottenbelt organised a mine visit so that we would know exactly what we were preparing ourselves for. We visited a Sasol mine called Syferfontein in Secunda, Mpumalanga. We were advised to arrive on campus very early one Friday morning. The buses left the campus at about 5 a.m.

We arrived at the main entrance of the mine and formed a queue: we were searched and had to blow into an alcohol detector. We all tested negative. We were then ushered into a big hall near the entrance. The mine manager, Themba Khumbaya, welcomed us, then asked, 'Where is Mr Knottenbelt?'

'Mr Knottenbelt went to Kriel – he escorted the other

half of the group,' said Mr Bukanga, the lecturer who had escorted us.

The mine manager continued, 'He was my lecturer when I was still in school in 1997.'

After concluding his boring speech, the manager handed over to the mine's safety officer. His name was Takalani; I forgot his surname. He demonstrated how to evacuate the mine should anything happen underground where we were going. He was very funny. After a few minutes, he was done.

A register was taken to keep a record of visitors entering and leaving the mine. We then went to the changing rooms and were given personal protective equipment (PPE), which included a safety harness, hard hat and battery lamp. We were transported to the mine in a mining car. We looked like cattle!

We arrived on site. The mine was a combination of a surface and an underground mine. I remember stepping into the mine. It felt like I was stepping onto the field of Lucas Moripe Stadium, where the benches were so beautiful. We met a miner, who welcomed us.

'I've been a miner for thirty-five years. I have seen it all,' he said, and started to give us another sermon. Luckily, he finished his history lesson before we got bored. He started to give us a tool-box talk, telling us the dos and don'ts of the workplace. 'We have a water problem,' he said, pointing to the ground. 'We wanted to dig further down, but we have a problem.'

I still remember the force of the ventilator blowing into our faces. We stepped into the cage to descend for one hundred and sixty metres and discover the harsh realities of coal mining, a clear view into the dangers and challenges faced by the men and women who toiled underground. I also still remember the darkness. It was like the first few seconds of load shedding that I used to experience in Mshongo. But there, it was worse. The sound of the unfiltered noise coming from equipment such as drills, crushers and engines broke down all communication and almost caused our eardrums to rupture. I relied only on the torch on my helmet in the darkness. We were all nearly wetting our pants from the experience of being underground. It was the first time that most of us had visited a mine. The reality that this was going to be our workplace after we graduated hit us. The miner's voice didn't change – he was one of the many who risked their lives by engaging in the deep, dark and dangerous business of mining. After going to different sections underground, we walked back to the cage and were hoisted back up. I had never been so happy to see the sun in my life.

We were transported back to the changing rooms. We showered and returned the PPE. We walked back to the hall, and we were served food. It was wonderful. The manager came back to give us his final remarks. 'Thank you for your visit to our mine. We also thank you for your cooperation throughout the day. Good luck with your studies. We are looking forward to working with some of you in the future.'

With those words, our visit to Syferfontein came to an end. We got back to campus at about 6 p.m. The following Monday, we attended our lectures knowing exactly what was ahead of us.

Campus was vibrant, filled with people from all walks of life. At times, it was a very hard place for me, though. As weird as it may sound, one thing that I discovered that depressed me more than anything else was that some students' allowances were greater than my mother's paycheque.

I started to reconsider going back to the pitch and playing varsity soccer. Sportsmen like Brian Habana and Lehlohonolo Majoro had nurtured their gifts while they were on campus. So, I thought I had a shot. But I quickly stopped playing soccer on campus – I realised that people who were not committed never accomplished much in class or even in life.

I became aware of the rivalry between Wits and UJ students, a rivalry that exists even today. Wits students considered themselves to be university students, while we were called 'the high school down the road'. Wits students were known for being smart, while UJ students were considered dumb – or Wits rejects. Wits was considered the Harvard of Africa. It had distinguished alumni, including Nelson Mandela. The institution had high minimum requirements, so it accommodated mostly learners from schools such as Waterkloof High, and a few outstanding students from segregated communities, like Katlego and Precious. (Wits is a Model C school for older people, though. Even its Katlegos and Preciouses can't stay very long; it's made for people who have money.)

This rivalry between the two universities, which faced each other, separated by the SABC offices in Auckland Park, was intense. Some of the students who had failed at Wits and come to UJ told us how tough Wits was. One such student was Charles Manaka. 'Wits is not child's play, *baba*. UJ is very easy,' he told me during one of Mr Knottenbelt's lectures in the new Perskor building. Each time I was tempted to respond, I had a conscious reminder that I, too, was a Wits reject. 'UJ doesn't produce thinkers. Wits students are smart, Chauke,' he continued. For that reason, I went through my entire university life knowing that I was intellectually inferior. Even after graduating, I felt incomplete, that I needed a reason to further my studies at Wits so I could be recognised as a graduate.

This UJ student vibe stayed with me in the workplace. The Wits students never regarded us as graduates, in the same way as white people never regard a black person as an educated person in any field of study. They always see a need to 'educate' the blacks, on all levels. Yet this in itself is the view of uneducated whites, mostly. Indeed, there may be no person on earth more ignorant than an uneducated white, who uses skin colour to put his or her agenda forward. You cannot deny me education, then call me inferior because I am unskilled. White people have undermined our intelligence, in the same way as they have told us that there is a place somewhere in the sky for us when we die.

But back to campus. I did not want to focus too much on the small matter of varsity feuds; I was determined to achieve excellence academically. I dreamt big and worked very hard to chase my dreams, knowing that humanity had a way of remembering its dreamers.

At Robin Crest, I became independent and took responsibility for myself. The lecturers did not monitor or follow up with us. There was no Mr Mathibela. I had to develop self-monitoring skills to keep up with the workload and the increased level of academic competition. I became assertive, and went out to seek assistance and support when I needed it. I became friends with Light Rikhotso, a senior mining student who stayed one block away from our apartment. Light gave me a bunch of old question papers. I applied myself, burning the midnight oil and spending most of my time in the study room and the library in John Orr. Poverty kept me up at night – the knowledge that I was poor was the main reason I was always studying. At the end of the first semester, I had done exceptionally well. They would usually display our exam results on the noticeboard. Most of my classmates started to notice me, since my name was at the top of the list.

By the second semester, Mr Knottenbelt was no longer my favourite lecturer. There was another lecturer, who lectured us in Engineering Work Study and Environmental Studies. His name was Ntabiso Ndiweni and he became my favourite. He was a Wits alumnus and he, too, would step in about the rivalry between UJ and Wits. Mr Ndiweni liked to emphasise that we *should* be thinkers.

Mr Ndiweni was very professional. He didn't have time to be friends with students, but I would always clown around in his class. One day, in an Environmental Studies class, he asked, 'Hey guys, what is groundwater?'

I raised my hand. 'Yes man,' he said, pointing at me.

'Groundwater is that water in Stjwetla in Alexandra,' I said.

The whole class laughed, and he joined them.

After class, he came up to me. 'Hey, man. Where are you from?' he asked.

'I am from Atteridgeville, sir.'

From that day, he started to recognise me. When he saw me in the hallways of John Orr, he would simply say, 'The man from Atteridgeville,' and I would turn around and greet him.

As I started to enjoy myself in Mr Ndiweni's class, I started to get along with other students as well. Some of them would ask me to help them with the modules they were having difficulty with. One day, as I was going to a lecture in Perskor, a young lady called my name. I did not recognise her. When she came up to me, I was embarrassed because I thought she was someone I should remember. We chatted for a while on our way to class.

'*Kambe vito ra wena hi wena mani?* (By the way, what's your name?)' I asked.

'*Hi mina Rinky* (My name is Rinky),' she answered.

We chatted for a while and she told me that she was from ka-Bungeni village, which was a few kilometres from my grandmother's home in Shirley. I started to get to know her. Sometimes, she would call me and ask if I could help her with work study. One day, she came with her roommate from their residence. We had sessions in Lwazi building, and I became friends with her friend as well. Both ladies clearly respected me, as I did them.

At the end of the academic year, my hard work had paid off. I was invited to the annual UJ awards on the main campus. I was among the first-year top achievers from the university's four campuses across all nine faculties.

I took a Mega Bus, which was part of the shuttle service that transported students between all four campuses, to the awards ceremony. I travelled to Auckland Park with my classmates Thuso Maimane and Emmanuel 'Magolide' Mosako. The bus passed Braamfontein. As I looked out the window, I saw the Wits Education campus. My heart broke seeing the university that had rejected me. But that didn't kill my excitement. From there, the bus stopped at the Bunting Road campus. Some students got off as others got on, en route to the main campus. We passed the SABC offices in Auckland Park and Campus Square, a shopping centre serving students who lived off campus. Immediately, we reached Kingsway Avenue, the road from which the main campus, Kingsway Campus, got its name. It ran along the north-east side of the campus.

We arrived at the parking lot on campus. As we got off the bus, we crossed a long bridge that offloaded us at Madibeng building, the university's main administration centre. It was a circular, concrete-and-steel building – basically one multipurpose structure, like Kalafong Hospital. We walked for about eight minutes into a long hallway, and passed all the sections of the building. Each section was about the same size as the seven-storey John Orr building. The sections were called rings – A ring, B ring, C ring, D ring and, finally, E ring, where the Sanlam Auditorium was located.

As we arrived at the thousand-seater auditorium, our tickets were taken and we were given our seat numbers. The auditorium also hosted concerts and graduation ceremonies. After a few minutes, all the students were inside. The whole SGB was welcomed and the UJ choir sang on the huge stage. The vice chancellor, Prof. Irhon Rensburg, and his two deputy vice chancellors, Prof. Tinyiko Maluleke and Prof. Tshilidzi Marwala, were in attendance. After they settled down, we sang the national anthem.

The programme started. Prof. Rensburg gave a wonderful speech. After his speech, we all lined up on the side of the hall, in the same way Jerry and his crew had lined up during their graduation. We stood in a place where many memories had been made by those who had come before us. This was a place where all UJ students were looking forward to being at the end of their painful years at the institution, and we were getting to ascend the stage in our first year already. Our faculty dean, Prof. Saurabh Sinha, called my name: 'Wisani Clinton Chauke.' I walked onto the stage, took my certificate and shook the vice chancellor's hand. I got an autograph from him. Then, I went to Prof. Maluleke, who was sitting next to Prof. Marwala. I asked for his autograph. Prof. Maluleke gave it to me, then looked at Prof. Marwala. They shared a smile.

I was filled with joy that day. When the event was over, we took pictures with members of the SGB and went outside. We took more pictures in front of the university's iconic fountains, then went back to Doornfontein. When I reached Robin Crest, I immediately called my father to tell him that I had got Prof. Maluleke's autograph. My father was very proud. '*Na ti nyungubyisa hi wena mfana mina* (I am proud of you, my boy),' he said.

Later in 2014, I also made it onto the Dean's Honour Roll in the Faculty of Engineering and the Built Environment. We were invited to breakfast with the dean of the faculty, Prof. Sinha.

When I got straight A's in my first year, I realised that I'd had the potential to be an A-student in high school – I'd just never had the resources. At UJ, I had Internet access, proper chairs and tables, all the stationery I needed, and a quiet environment. And, I didn't have to go to a JoJo tank. In high school, I was forced to produce mediocre results because of the conditions at home – a common trend, indeed, in poor families. If I'd had access to resources at school, maybe I would have shaken Angie Motshekga's hand, just as Mr Mangena had prophesied.

As Malcolm X said, 'When you live in a poor neighbourhood, you are living in an area where you have poor schools. When you have poor schools, you have poor teachers. When you have poor teachers, you get a poor education. When you get a poor education, you can only work in a poor-paying job. And that poor-paying job enables you to live again in a poor neighbourhood. So, it's a very vicious cycle.'

Chapter 20

An experiment in love

At varsity, nobody really studies your movements. But, due to the crazy things I used to do in Mr Ndiweni's class, almost everybody in our class knew me. I used to wear formal clothes a lot. Most of the time, I dressed like an executive but ultimately behaved like I was in kindergarten. My presence was very hard to ignore and, at times, annoying. I just didn't care. If you liked me, it was cool. If you didn't, it was not a big deal.

I began losing my innocence with girls. There were beautiful girls on our campus, but they were not as beautiful as the ones on the main campus. Our campus was mostly for engineering students, so the female students didn't really have time for make-up or to follow fashion trends. But there was a girl I loved. Her name was Basani Sambo. She was friends with Rinky, the girl I used to help with her work.

I met Basani for the first time in a group meeting for a presentation in our Communication class. I used to be good at presentations. '*Clinton, nikombela u hi joiner ka group ya hina?* (Clinton, can you join us in our group?)' Rinky had asked. I joined them to make a group of five. It was me, a guy named John Matsimane, Salome Chauke,

Rinky and Basani. The three girls were friends and they were all Vatsonga.

I still remember the first time I met Basani. Her beauty struck me and I knew right then that she would be my partner at some stage. She smiled genuinely and expressed anger genuinely. She didn't look like any of the Hollywood stars. She was no Beyoncé or Angelina Jolie. Basani was far from perfect, but in my heart she was.

We met at John Orr to prepare for our presentation. '*Kunjhani?* (How are you?)' I greeted.

'*Ni kona kunjhani?* (I'm fine, and you?)' she replied

'*Kambe wena u huma kwihi?* (Where are you from?)' I asked.

We chatted for a while, then our conversation melted away. After the meeting, we all exchanged numbers. '*Ni nyike ta wena, ntaku founela kunene Wisani* (Wisani, rather give me your contact number. I will call you),' she said.

At UJ, we called each other by our surnames. Very few people knew my first names. So, when she called me by my first name, Wisani, it made me feel very special.

From that point, we communicated mostly on WhatsApp. She would frequently visit her mother on the weekends in Katlehong, where she also attended the Faith Mission Church. She loved church like my sister Tsakani, was a little stubborn like Akani, and her strength was almost equal to that of my mother. I was mesmerised to see all the qualities of the people I'd grown up with in my house combined in one person. I could see that she loved her family dearly. I liked her because she was

191

also Mutsonga. My mother always advised, '*Loko u teka, u teka mutsonga* (When you get married, make sure it's a Tsonga woman).'

All my crushes were always carefully controlled. This means they never knew about my feelings for them. But Basani made my heart skip a bit. I couldn't control it. Kamogelo Makeketlane was the one who noticed that I'd fallen for Basani, before I'd even known it. We were walking from class and we bumped into Basani at the library in John Orr. They went into the library and I waited outside. I was waiting for Kamogelo to print out an assignment, and became impatient.

'Hey, man. You are wasting my time,' I confronted him when he was done.

Kamogelo replied, 'Basani said I should tell you not to worry because I was still talking to her.'

I quickly blushed. It was funny how I moved from angry to giggling in a second at the mention of Basani. Makeketlane realised that, as much as I liked Basani, she liked me.

I remember, soon after writing exams, how we glanced at each other in the hallway. She came running to me with both arms open. She hugged me so tightly, her small breasts pressing against my chest. I could feel her heartbeat. The only thing I was thinking was her in my bedroom, but I remembered that we were devoted to our religion. I immediately released her from my arms, but she held on to me, almost like she was resting on my body. When we finally ended the hug, I could see the love in her eyes. They were glowing, almost teary. It was the first time I had seen all the signs of a girl liking you at once. My heart was beating so fast.

We went our separate ways.

From that point, my love for her intensified, but I was afraid of her. The deeper my feelings towards her became, the more I ignored her. And she kept on coming to me. Girls love guys who don't give them the time, I guess.

One day, she confronted me: 'Why are you always ignoring me, *kasi*?'

She was very smart. I realised later that, even though she never uttered the words 'I love you,' she did a lot of things to demonstrate her love to me. She guided me and comforted me, but I was always rushing – and, ultimately, had no clue about how to handle her.

I had a very bad habit of laughing at almost anything. She called me out for it: '*He Wisani tshika mhaka ya wena leyo tshama u kha u hlekelela* (Wisani, let go of your habit of laughing at almost everything).'

I responded, 'But there's nothing wrong *hiku hleka mus* (But there's nothing wrong with laughing).'

She disagreed. 'Imagine we are walking down the aisle and the pastor says kiss the bride and you are there giggling.'

Basani had a way of making me see the bigger picture.

She introduced me to Celine Dion. I started to understand her through Celine Dion's music. 'Just walk away' was her favourite song. You know, girls have different 'favourite songs', depending on a guy. People always misunderstood her, but I understood her better than she understood herself. I was the king of analysing people.

As I got used to her love and attention, I started to get cocky. I bragged about my abilities, always making it known that I was among the top achievers. Before I could seal the deal with Basani, she rejected me. In fact, she rejected me before our first date. It was not really a date, but let's call it a date, because we went to McDonald's. I picked her up at her residence, which was on campus.

She began to study me intensively from the first moment we made contact. I gave her a hug, at which she immediately said, 'That is not how you hug a lady. You must hug me with two hands.'

She put me into challenge mode from that point: I wanted to prove myself.

We took a ten-minute walk to McDonald's, which was very close to Ellis Park Stadium. We talked about religion; it was a time when I was starting to have my own understanding of my religion. I was defining what religion meant in my life and was very sceptical about the idea of having a pastor. But Basani was a strong follower of the pastors.

'There is no such a thing as a pastor,' I said. I had read a scripture where Jesus said that he was the only pastor, and that everyone who claimed to be a pastor was just a deceiver. I went on with my rant. I talked about how tithing was wrong. I talked about how good I was at everything that I did. By the time we got to the restaurant, she knew everything about me.

When we got to the restaurant, she was the one who

ordered the food and she also offered to pay. When our order arrived, I took our tray and immediately started going upstairs.

'Why do you want to hide? Everyone is hiding up there,' she said.

We sat down and began to eat. At a table next to us, there were two guys who were busy on their laptops. It looked like they had come for the Wi-Fi. I was dominating our conversation in every way possible. It is true that women mature faster than men; Basani was way ahead of me. My inexperience in love was my downfall. She saw that when she tried to hold my hand and I quickly pulled away. It was not that I didn't love her – my whole life, I'd been told that girls love guys who had good looks and money, and I was insecure because I had neither. Basani was not into all those things; she was genuinely interested in my heart, the one I refused to give her. At that McDonald's table, I struggled with my posture and I couldn't even maintain eye contact with her. I mean, if I couldn't look deep into her eyes, into her soul, how was I going to make love to her? Seeing all this, Basani quickly called our meeting off.

We left that restaurant. On our way out, I begged her to go back and try our conversation again. She agreed. We now sat at a table outside the restaurant. It was in the centre, and looked like it had been prepared for the two of us. On our left, there were two ladies who looked like they were friends and on our right, there was a couple who were a little older than us. They were engaged in a serious romantic conversation.

I continued where I had left off, continuing to be cocky and talkative. I remember she was telling me about her friend who had been in a relationship with a guy for a long period of time, and then found out that she was a side chick.

I quickly interrupted her and said, loudly, 'Well, in my matric year, I had a girlfriend. She became pregnant during our relationship and we never had sex.'

Basani was embarrassed. She quickly glanced at the two ladies on our left and at the couple on our right. Then she erupted into laughter. She had looked at them almost as an invitation to laugh at the clown who was in front of her.

I didn't laugh. She called it quits. The worst part is that the bold statement I had made was a lie. I had never had a girlfriend.

The whole time, I'd been speaking English. I wanted to sound cool and smart, but what a turn-off! She asked me why I was speaking English, since we were Vatsonga. I replied, 'I've learnt the language of my oppressors.'

She laughed sarcastically.

I continued to talk down to her. I treated her like an obstacle to be overcome, rather than an individual I was supposed to love. I failed to realise that all the things I was doing were signs of insecurity. She was a year older than me. I'd said that age was not an issue and I wanted to believe it. But, painful as it was, my immaturity was my downfall. I never took the time to listen to a single word she said. I knew that we had a lot in common, but I didn't agree with any of the things she suggested.

'My dream house is in Sandton,' she said.

I said I didn't like Sandton, and preferred Polokwane. I mean, who doesn't want to stay in Sandton? All the rich people in South Africa live in Sandton.

Seeing all these things, she made up her mind and called the meeting off, like she'd done before. Basani realised that I was a deeply flawed person who had a lot of unfinished business, but she also realised that I was not humble enough to accept this about myself. She was neither ready nor willing to help me through my internal issues. She said to me, 'You know what, Wisani? I was infatuated with you.' Looking deep into my eyes, she realised that this was too much for me. Then, 'Wisani,' she said, 'learn to accept rejection. Be glad that we never made memories and I never knew you that well.'

I couldn't hide my need to be loved and admired from Basani, but my ego won, and I lost her in the process. I was broken. I had seen myself marrying her. I was really looking forward to meeting her mother and giving her a handshake – and probably a hug – for raising such a strong woman, but my dream of going to Katlehong had faded away.

I tried to get answers from my buddy Makekektlane about where I'd got it wrong with Basani. 'Don't ever tell a woman you love her in the early days, especially when you are still pursuing her. She knows how you feel about her. Just show her how well you can take care of her,' he responded.

I wanted to let go, as she told me to do, but I realised that the state of being in love doesn't just fade away that quickly. I struggled to deal with Basani's rejection; in this way, dear reader, I discovered my own hypocrisy. I realised that I was just a regular person, that there was nothing special about me.

Nothing.

Chapter 21

UJ: Second year

Backed by good grades in my first year and my ability to speak many languages, I had a reputation to maintain in my second year. But the challenges also started to escalate. In the course that I was doing, before I could do third year, I needed to do practical training in a mine. The course content of the third year was based on that training. After failing to find a company where I could do practical training, I was left with a choice: sit at home, or take a risk and go back to varsity to learn the content that would be difficult to process. The senior students told me that it would be difficult, and that I faced the possibility of getting an academic exclusion.

I took a big risk and continued with my studies.

It almost didn't happen. The year before, I hadn't applied for NSFAS on time and I didn't have a bursary. Every student could relate to me about this. They could give you 365 days to do an assignment, and you would only do it when it was due the following day. Anyway, I could not submit my NSFAS application because there was an outstanding document. Was it not degrading, though, that before you got help, you had to prove that you were poor? I think it was fair but degrading nonetheless. I couldn't get a document for my father's disability grants. Ultimately, I failed to submit my NSFAS application.

At the beginning of the year, I begged my mother to borrow money from my aunt, Conny Baloyi. Aunt Conny lent me R6 337 for registration at school and residence at Robin Crest.

I was no longer as optimistic as I had been when I started my first year. I was no longer interested in the academic competition. I had teamed up with a guy called Muhluri Shirinda. We were the two clowns of the class. Shirinda was crazy, but he had a good heart. He would even share his food with me when I got stuck during the year.

On campus, I was a floater and a clown. I moved effortlessly from one group to another. I could relate very well to my fellow Vatsonga students from Giyani; some of them even didn't believe that I stayed in Atteridgeville. I took my coolness from Saulridge to another level, for I was born in a township, had stayed in a village, and grew up in a squatter camp. I knew both worlds, so it was easier for me to interact with almost every student on campus.

I could have a productive conversation with a Pedi lady. I could speak about traditional music with a guy from KwaZulu-Natal and discuss initiation school with a young man from the Eastern Cape. When I spoke Tshivenda, I fitted in very well because of my skin tone. I could also relate well to kids from Model C schools. Using my humour, I would socialise with on-campus pastors, then have a meaningful conversation with the security guards, talk fitness training with the gym guys, then discuss computers with the geeks. But my favourite group was the politically conscious ones.

I remember, shortly after Julius Malema had visited our campus to mobilise for the Economic Freedom Fighters (EFF), I was chilling with some of the SRC guys (Lucas Mapeyi and Thabo Maphuthuma) in the student centre close to the gate. These guys always revealed something I did not know. Lucas turned to me and said, 'Look at you, Chauke. Now, after you graduate, you will go and work. And most probably someone is going to lend you money for a house and maybe a car. What is the point of saying you own a house or car if those things are going to be bound by the bank? If you get fired, the house or car will return to its owners.'

I thought he was pushing it too far, but I agreed that the concept of ownership was very important. I thought ownership was a very powerful thing, because it brought pride. I heard it in the voice of our neighbour, who owned a shack. He told anyone who would not mind his or her own business that 'This is my yard. Don't come here and tell me what to do in my own yard!' The thought of our being tenants, rather than owners, was engrained in the minds of both my parents' generation and the so-called born-frees.

I supported Lucas by also revealing that we were comfortable with *go berekela lekhowa* (working for a white man). We associated good things with white people, and undermined ourselves. This had been the real objective of apartheid. Even though apartheid has ended, a new generation of young black people still undermines itself, because their minds are not yet emancipated from apartheid. This sense of inferiority, deliberately cultivated by the structures of white power during apartheid, is still prevalent today. You can see it in small things, like when we repeatedly and shamefully correct one another if we don't know a Western norm or aspect of culture, when we laugh at one another savagely when someone can't speak proper English, or when we are too embarrassed to listen to our traditional music.

I also indicated to the two gentlemen that, according to data and statistics, black South Africans were poor compared to their white counterparts. I could not claim to Lucas that I had a relationship with any white people. I mean, in South Africa, you would hardly find a white person living in a shack or a township. Even there, on campus, they were always isolated from us and we made no effort to connect with them, partly because we did not believe that being friends with a person of another race was an achievement.

But I was not too naïve to admit that some white people have also been brutally attacked by poverty – people who struggle to pay their bills and are deprived of certain services because of black economic empowerment (BEE). Indeed, a walk through Munsieville, a white squatter camp in Krugersdorp, is not unlike a walk through Mshongo. But, when we analyse our problems, we do so collectively – not based on a small, individual sample. We can't take Patrice Motsepe as an example and start generalising that blacks are rich. Rather, we analyse the whole population. Collectively, black people have been the victims of poverty; collectively, white people are privileged. Period.

Thabo quickly joined in and emphasised my point. He also suggested that varsity was useless. I obviously disagreed with him, because I loved varsity very much. I fully agreed that we could never apply Charles Darwin's theory to paying our electricity bills, or Lame's theorem to solving serious, real-life problems, but I believed that education really opened people's minds, allowing them to think objectively in different dimensions, and encouraged critical thinking and problem solving.

But, after a heated debate with Thabo about the topic of education, I finally agreed that a mere university degree would not do me any good in life. His argument was that, at varsity, they did not teach us how to think: they taught us what to think. So, to some extent, it became pointless. I thought self-education was key, but since we did not have the resources, we could not access the information we needed. I revealed to the two gentlemen that it was only after I got to varsity that I had access to YouTube for the first time. I was conflicted because I thought education was important, but the current educational system didn't speak to the experiences of someone from my background. At the end of our discussion, I still maintained that people would not admit it, but education was a gateway to opportunities. In this highly competitive world, the only thing you could sell was your knowledge.

Outside the classroom, most of my peers did not really see how hard I was trying to reconcile my past with my present. Because of all the contradictions that life had thrown at me, and the shame that came with staying in a shack, whenever I met new people on campus, I always struggled to explain where I was really from. I tried to blend in with everyone, behaving like a chameleon.

It was not only on campus. In Atteridgeville, people always asked, '*Hey o ya neng gae Giyani?* (Hey, when are you going to your native home in Giyani?)' My father always reminded me that '*La, a hile kaya, a kaya hile ka Bevhula* (This is not home. Home is in Bevhula).' When I claimed Elim to be my home, my aunt quickly told me how foolish I was to regard my mother's home as my own. When I finally came back to my senses and went to my father's home ka-Bevhula, as I walked around the village, all I could hear was, '*Ah I magayisa ya le Joni naa* (Oh, the visitors from Johannesburg),' or '*Hayi u tshama joni loyi* (No, this one stays in Johannesburg).'

I found myself in an in-between space, not fitting in anywhere. The problem of being a chameleon is the main reason that I can now come out of the closet and reject the born-free label.

I cannot change my colours to pretend I am free.

During holidays, I would visit home. I travelled to or from varsity by train and, since there was quite a distance between Johannesburg and Pretoria, I found myself laughing every time the train passed through Knights Station – at how I looked at the squatter camps, just a few feet from the station. I laughed at how I acted as if it was the first time I had seen something like a squatter camp. I felt bad for the people staying there, but in truth, I was just like them.

One of the things I liked when I met friendly strangers on the train was to talk and listen to them, I would ask where they came from and where they were going. During one of my journeys, as the train stopped at Oakmoor station, in walked a man; we got to talking about the Soweto derby that was to be played later that day. He asked who I was and where I was going. I proceeded, and introduced myself. I told him that I was a university student. You know, when you are a student, you always feel a need to tell everybody who you are and what you are doing. In return, he introduced himself and also stated that he was a student. 'I have studied in the best university of them all,' he said. I anticipated the name of the university. But, 'I studied in the University of Life,' he concluded.

At that point, I knew I was going to get the best wisdom from him, so I prepped myself. He asked me a very easy question: 'What do you want in life?'

I said, 'What kind of question is that?'

He replied, 'It is the kind of question you have to answer right now.'

I realised I did not know what I wanted from my life.

'Until you know what you want in life,' he said, 'you have not started to live.'

I will not lie, he provoked my thoughts.

I liked using the train a lot, because it was cheap. There was always drama on the train, and I would see different types of characters. In the train, I also observed some subtle aspirations – and difficulties – that people shared. I saw the hopefulness in the eyes of parents standing on a packed train, believing that, maybe, if they could go on just a little bit more, their children might relieve them one day by getting ahead in life. When the announcer on the public address system said 'All change' for the third time, I would watch as broken spirits dragged their broken bodies to the next platform. I would share in their pain.

I thought I was the only person having a tough time in life until I visited one of my friends, John Mabe, who stayed in the infamous Ponte City. He was always behind in school work, so I asked him what was wrong. He told me that he was working part-time as a waiter to pay his tuition fees. He would sleep for three hours before he started night shift, so he had little time to study. When I got back to res, I thought about him in my room. I imagined him waiting tables, having to fake a smile or laugh at a customer's stupid remarks, using broken English, taking orders for things he did not know, and having customers walk out after complaining that the food was cold and having to pay their bill. After doing all that, he had to get back home and focus on his all-consuming course of study. I regained some strength from his story; it made me push even harder.

Since our institution was formerly predominately white, I was encouraged when I walked around and saw more black faces. The weapons for fighting poverty were at our disposal. But I was often puzzled by the students who acted as if they did not know poverty. Using the money they got from their bursaries, they would hide behind their designer clothes, change their accents, and completely forget about where they came from.

I studied for the whole year without paying the university, so I was in debt. I was very hungry for success. But, during that year, I was physically hungry, too. It was difficult to study and do well when you had an empty stomach and, added to that, were not going to see your results at the end of the semester. I knew that I was paying the price of fitting into previously white spaces that had suddenly become accessible 'for all'.

This is the problem that born-frees face today: we try so hard to access these white spaces, but staying in them seems like mission impossible. In the end, I had to write two supplementary exams. This didn't sit well with me, moving from being a top achiever to a supplementary student.

I was very frustrated.

Chapter 22

#FeesMustFall

I was not the only student experiencing the frustration of university fees. A lot of students were in a similar situation. Growing up, we were told that we could be anything we wanted to be, but then we realised that we had to pay for it. The goalposts had been moved. We observed that, when a country sells something that is supposed to be basic, like education, it becomes self-defeating. When you put a price tag on anything, you invite inequality. Where there was a price tag, there would always be class.

We finally decided to stand up and raise our concerns using the hashtag #FeesMustFall. The protests started at the 'real' university, Wits, and spread to ours. Wits students rejected the 10.5 per cent university fee increase proposed by the minister of higher education, Blade Nzimande.

I still remember the day it started on our campus. I was in my room at Robin Crest and I heard chanting and singing outside. I thought it was the normal call of *vimba*. But the singing grew louder and louder. I then went outside, onto the balcony, and realised that whatever the occasion might be, it was huge.

'The guys are protesting against the university fees,' my roommate Lebogang Maphuthuma told me. I started to have hope that my debt might be cancelled. I quickly jumped into the lift, went all the way down to the ground floor, and joined the guys on Saratoga Avenue.

We marched all the way to Braamfontein, where we met up with Wits students. For the first time, the Wits students acknowledged that we were also university students. It was beautiful to see the students in solidarity. Even the white students joined us. Solidarity was crucial in our cause.

Our protest was aligned with #RhodesMustFall, demanding the removal of the Cecil Rhodes statue at the University of Cape Town. Their campaign had spread across the country and demanded that my favourite statue at Church Square be removed. I didn't believe that taking statues of dead white men down would bring me any justice. Yes, those statues represented centuries of ancestral pride, but taking them down wouldn't ensure equality in this country. As for me, I was focused on the elephant in our room. Like #RhodesMustFall, our campaign also spread across the country. We were organised. It was said that we were all going to Pretoria to demonstrate at the Union Buildings, where the president was scheduled to address us.

On 23 October 2015, I woke up very early in the morning and, with my friend John Mabe, I took a Mega Bus from campus and headed to Pretoria, my hometown. We arrived at Madiba Street and joined thousands of other students who were singing and chanting, holding up placards reading 'Fees Must Fall'. Songs and singing have always been a centrepiece of the African people. When we were happy, we sang. When we were sad, we sang. When we protested, we also sang, and had been doing so since the pre-1994 struggle years.

From Madiba Street, we marched – and others danced – to the big lawn outside the Union Buildings. We marched on the same streets that the women of 1956 had marched on. I could feel their strength; having grown up in a household of women, and continuing to be surrounded by them, I knew the power they represented and how resilient they were. When the guys started singing, 'My mother was a kitchen girl, my father was a garden boy, that's why I am a communist!' it almost reduced me to tears. It reminded me of my own parents.

The struggle songs raised our spirits higher, but one song in particular energised us: '*Iyho uSolomon*'. It was the leading song on that October day. '*Iyho uSolomon*' was a praise song for struggle hero Solomon Mahlangu. This was a great change of pace: for centuries, on the African continent, we have been taught to praise and worship someone who was humble and forgiving and non-violent. I guess you know who I'm talking about. So, in Madiba Street, we stepped forward with our arms stretched out, then gave a huge clap like we did at His Rest.

'*Iyhoooooooooooooooooooooo! uSolomon! So-lo-mone! Iyho-ooooooooooooooooooo! uSolomon! Waye yisotsha, Iso-tsha lo-uMkhonto weSizwe! Wayo bulala amabhunu eAfrika!* (Oh Solomon! The uMkhonto weSizwe [Spear of the Nation] soldier who killed the Boers in Africa!)'

Solomon was born not far away from where we were, in the township of Mamelodi. He died at the age of twenty-two. He had left the country when he was nineteen to be trained as an uMkhonto weSizwe soldier in Mozambique and Angola. He came back to the country through Swaziland in 1977 carrying guns, grenades and ANC pamphlets. Entering a taxi rank in Johannesburg to take the taxi to Soweto to commemorate the June 16 student uprising, he was stopped by the apartheid government police. He panicked. Shots were fired. Some onlookers were shot dead, and others injured. Solomon was charged for murder under provisions of the Terrorism Act of 1967.

On 6 April 1979, the date on which Jan van Riebeeck had arrived in South Africa in 1652, Solomon was sent to be hanged at Pretoria Central Prison. His hanging caused an international scene. The police decided to bury Solomon in Atteridgeville, afraid that there would be violent protests if his funeral were held in Mamelodi.

The late ANC president Oliver Tambo said this of Solomon Mahlangu, while delivering the 'Spirit of Bandung' speech in Lusaka: 'In his brief but full life Solomon Mahlangu towered like a colossus, unbroken and unbreakable, over the fascist lair. He, on whom our people have bestowed accolades worthy of the hero-combatant that he is, has been hanged in Pretoria like a common murderer. Alone the hangmen buried Solomon, bound by a forbidding oath that his grave shall remain forever a secret, because, in his death the spirit of Solomon Mahlangu towers still like a colossus, unbroken and unbreakable, over the fascist lair.'

In April 1993, Solomon's body was reinterred at the Mamelodi Cemetery, where his most famous and inspiring quote was inscribed on his tomb: 'My blood will nourish the tree that will bear fruits of freedom. Tell my people that I love them. They must continue the fight.'

The song brought out the brave side of each student at the Union Buildings on that day.

In the crowd, I heard one of our students say, 'The youth of 1976 have betrayed the youth of 2015.' That made me think hard: the people who were in power had been in the struggle yesterday. Higher education minister Blade Nzimande had provoked us earlier, before the march. In a press conference, he had been caught on camera, joking that, 'If the students don't accept this, we'll start our own movement, #StudentsMustFall,' before bursting out laughing. His comments may have been light-hearted and intended as a joke, but we didn't have time to laugh. #StudentsMustFall trended immediately. Although we had taken our inspiration from the youth of 1976, that student was right: they *had* betrayed us. They looked like they were clueless about our attempts to end our deprivations.

We continued singing at the Union Buildings until some small mobile toilets were set on fire. Helicopters started hovering over us, dropping teargas bombs and shooting rubber bullets and stun grenades. Some of our students started forcing their way beyond the barricades to the Union Buildings. Police nyalas, which had been on standby, started driving up and down, trying to contain the students.

President Zuma was scheduled to address us after his meeting with vice chancellors and SRCs. In the afternoon, a zero per cent fee increase for the 2016 academic year fees was announced live on national TV instead.

The outcome of the meeting was good for some students, but not for me. My debt still stood. What I wanted to achieve from the march was to see my debt scrapped, along with all the historical debt dating back to the year in which I was born: these debts, coupled with black tax, were the real challenges prohibiting us young blacks from making a meaningful contribution to the economy. Since my debt still stood, I would automatically be excluded from the university. The outcome of the meeting was a failure to bring about free, decolonised education. We had failed to dismantle the anti-black system that maintained black oppression in our time. President Zuma even failed to come and address us. I was angry because I hadn't seen him.

As soon as the announcement was made, I took John around the city. By the time we got back to the Union Buildings, the Mega Buses had left us behind. We took the taxi known as 'Pheli-Via-Church' to my home in Atteridgeville.

I have never been as embarrassed in my life as I was that day. My home was not as beautiful as the houses I'd been showing John around town. It was worse because there was no electricity that day at home. But John was a cool guy. He didn't have a problem with where I lived. He was just fascinated by the living conditions of Mshongo.

'Wow, man. How did you get to UJ from staying in a place like this?' he asked me.

It was a question I couldn't answer; I just didn't have the energy. The following day, we took a taxi and went back to school in Johannesburg. Later, it was reported that the protest had been the first major demonstration by students since the 1976 Soweto uprising. We had been part of that history.

Marching in the streets of Pretoria, demanding fees to fall, had been very personal for me. I was angry: I was entering adulthood without a proper roof over my head, which meant that I was entering adulthood without financial security. I then asked myself: What does it mean to be young and black in South Africa? When the mind asks tough questions, the heart feels pain. Being young and black in South Africa was about being young and broke, I answered myself. I figured out that hustling should become my trademark. Look, money is not everything – but it makes a huge difference.

As a black person, all you have to do is worry about finding a 'mature' partner, securing a home loan, making babies, managing debit orders, tolerating your racist boss, going to church and listening to its lies, and getting a life policy. And then you die. Chains! Chains! Everywhere! There is no time to live.

People always looked shocked when they saw us black people angry. They were puzzled, as if they did not know where our anger came from. They got irritated when they saw the Pikitup cleaners striking and leaving the entire city stinking. They did not understand it when students

214

burned auditoriums. They could not comprehend it when a young fellow resorted to criminal means to make ends meet.

While I was an angry person by default – my circumstances had made me a bitter person – I did not believe that violence was a solution. Destroying schools or school facilities only added more social problems. But I did acknowledge that violence was the only language that the guys in power seemed to understand. When the voices of the poor were being constantly silenced, violence was supposed to be a solution.

I think that the inequalities that govern born-frees' lives can be addressed, but certainly not in our lifetime. The focus of some of the 'educated' ones is heavenward; they forget that they are on earth. Religion has robbed them of their intelligence.

Chapter 23

They hate racism, but fully embrace tribalism

Witnessing violence during #FeesMustFall was not a new thing for me. It was normal; in the squatter camp, we were always on strike. If it was not about service delivery, then it was about corruption. If not corruption, then crime.

Violence and strikes had become part of my DNA. Except when it was xenophobic violence. During the xenophobic attacks in 2008, I was terrified. The attackers did not distinguish between me, a Shangaan with a very dark complexion, and their actual targets.

When the violence reached its peak, I would even not go to school. Witnessing the fatal stabbing of a Mozambican man who stayed two streets away from my home made me scared. I thought I could die at any time – everybody who did not belong to the dominant ethnic groups – Zulu, Tswana and Xhosa – was attacked. My fellow South Africans also viewed members of smaller groups like mine as foreigners. We 'looked foreign' and were 'too dark' to be South Africans. White people were not viewed as foreigners in the context of xenophobic violence, however. Not a single white immigrant was killed during the attacks. The attacks were black on black. I hate to say this about us, but we have been taught to hate each other.

South Africa, considered the most industrialised country on the continent, attracted foreign nationals from countries like Zimbabwe, Mozambique, Ethiopia and Somalia. These were people who were struggling in their own countries. The attacks on these foreigners started in Alexandra township and soon reached Atteridgeville. Violence and looting that targeted foreigners and their businesses erupted in the usual spot, the taxi rank in Maunde Street. The attackers burned spaza shops owned by foreign nationals – Africans in particular.

The attacks were concentrated in the squatter camps, where a lot of angry black people resided. They gave different reasons for the attacks. Some foreigners were blamed for their businesses taking away customers; others were blamed for competing with locals for scarce resources. The attacks were both verbal and physical. The victims were called derogatory names. '*Makwere-kwere a tshwenya, a tsamaye, ba re tseyela mmereko waitsi* (These foreigners are problematic. They must go. They take away our jobs),' I would often hear on the streets. But, as I meticulously assessed the attacks, I noticed that they were selectively targeted at Zimbabweans, despite the presence of other foreign nationals in our area, like people from Botswana and Lesotho. The reason for this was that the Zimbabweans were very dark compared to the other foreigners. Many of their houses were burned down. Their shops were looted, and some were burned down with their owners still inside them. The government deployed the army. Nyalas like the ones at #FeesMustFall moved up and down our squatter camp.

During the attacks, I realised that being a Shangaan was a curse.

Because of the stigma that came with being a Mutsonga, I had always thought it was absurd for someone who was Mutsonga to be on TV because of the way we were treated in society. When I saw people like David Mathebula wearing the Kaizer Chiefs jersey or Tonic Chabalala rocking the Buccaneers jersey, I was fascinated. I would also be fascinated watching Mbhazima Shilowa, the premier of Gauteng, and Tito Mboweni, the governor of the South African Reserve Bank, on TV. And these two fascinated me more: unlike David and Tonic, the soccer players, or Thomas, Benny and Madjozi, who were musicians and entertainers, Mbhazima and Tito were famous for being smart! In black society, a Mutsonga or Shangaan is always seen as someone who is barbaric, uncivilised and very stupid. Even in fictional shows such as *Generations* or *Muvhango*, you will never see an intelligent Mutsonga. The only time you will see a Mutsonga on TV is when they show a stupid one.

It always hit me how my fellow Africans hated racism, but fully embraced tribalism. To me, it was the same thing: discriminating against another group of people because they were different from you in some way. The profiling in the case of racism is on the basis of race; in tribalism, it is on the basis of tribe.

I remember how a Tswana family treated me when I was tutoring their child during my gap year. They all liked my attitude, and it was out of their liking for me that I soon became accepted by them. After all, I was helping their baby girl with mathematics.

They would talk about everything the same way people would talk freely in front of a parrot. They talked about *mashangaan* as if I could not understand them. I remember one day when Mr Phala, as nice as he was, came in from Selbourne Side, where he had been through the Vatsonga section, and said to Mrs Sebola, right in front of me: '*A ke boni gore why machangani a le a rasa so ale badidi so* (I just can't see how those Shangaans can be so noisy while being so poor).' He talked about how they wore expensive clothes, but lived in shacks and rented houses. Mrs Sebola said, with me standing right there, '*Machangani a beyao abuti* (Shangaans are just that way, my brother).'

That scene has always stayed with me.

I was angry because they did not give me credit for having the same talents that they would have been ready and willing to recognise in a Tswana boy in my position. Even at UJ, I experienced the same discrimination. Provident Molete, our class rep, was one of the culprits. He would usually talk about *mashangaan* in derogatory terms. Provident never saw us as people. His favourite lines were, '*Ntwe ke lechangani* (This thing is a Shangaan),' and '*Machangani a so* (Shangaans are that way).' He would never associate himself with a Shangaan. I found his behaviour disturbing, because he was a very

219

smart young man. But his mind was as thoroughly enslaved as our grandparents' minds had been during apartheid.

Historically, Batswana have never seen us as people – Batswana are generally very light-skinned, so a Motswana asserts the same superiority over a Mutsonga as a white man does over a black man in this country.

It was not only Provident who discriminated against me in Johannesburg. I was stopped more than once on the streets of Johannesburg during my varsity days by the police, who usually stopped foreigners in their stop-and-search operations. These operations profiled people and made negative assumptions about them. I remember going to Johannesburg Park Station one day. A female police officer came to me and said in broken English, 'Hey my brother, how are you?' Knowing that this was usually the start of a rant that would result in my having to produce my legal documents, I replied her in Zulu so she would think I was South African.

'*Ngiya phila kunjani ses wam?* (I'm good, and you, my sister?) I replied.

She didn't buy into my Zulu. In her broken English, she continued, 'Can I search your bag?'

I gave her my bag. She searched savagely and left most of my belongings displaced. Without closing my bag, she said, 'Can I see your passport?'

We both knew that I looked foreign because I was 'too dark' to be South African. That I could easily take: I've been called worse names on soccer fields and in mines. But what was really disturbing was her utter arrogance.

Frustrated, I asked, 'Why *u funa i* passport *yam?* (Why do you want my passport?)'

'You can't come over here without a passport,' she replied.

I said I didn't have a passport. '*Ngi phete* student card *kuphela* (I only have my student card).'

She shrugged, and walked away. 'Next time, carry your passport.'

I remembered that my own grandfather, who had contributed greatly to building Johannesburg into what it was, was himself required to carry a passbook. The passbook came to be known as the *dompas*; people who were caught without it could be thrown out of urban areas and deported back to their homelands. I was very angry. I noticed it then: the Republic was in peril. There was confusion all over the land.

Since we were the most despised group in the mad society we lived in, we were closely united: we had only one another. I remember, once, visiting my cousin, Treasure Vilankulu, who stayed in Tembisa on the East Rand. As I was randomly walking in the streets, a very dark-skinned man overheard me talking on the phone. The next question I got was, '*Se mi huma kwihi kaya bot?* (Where are you from, brother?)'

That is how I wished South Africa could have been: that united.

I started to believe that some of us, our minds were still colonised. For as long as we were still calling each other names like *leShangane* or *makwapa* or *magrigamba* or *makwerekwere*, we were unconsciously deepening

221

the wounds of apartheid. When we allowed tribalism to divide our country, we scratched open the scars of apartheid.

We needed to do as Bob Marley warned when he quoted Marcus Garvey in 'Redemption Song', I thought. We needed to emancipate ourselves from mental slavery.

'None but ourselves can free our minds' . . .

Chapter 24

Verwoerd succeeded

My second year at UJ flew. Still, I did not have practical training. I then decided to look for a job: I could not afford to go back to the shack that I called home back in Atteridgeville. I recalled the pain of sitting at home during my gap year, and was frustrated, and feared that I would get addicted to drugs just to find solace from my problems. I have seen many good people falling victim to that.

I was also afraid of going home and having people suggest that I apply for a driver's licence. We were living in a society that taught us that it was more important to have a driver's licence than an education. That, to me, always suggested that it was better to be a taxi driver than to go to school. *What was the point of getting a driver's licence if I was not going to own my own car anytime soon?* I asked myself. As much as I was trying to avoid the traps that were ahead of me, I also did not have many options. If I could get a job, it would keep me busy. I went job hunting.

I realised that I had come of age when I went to find a job and nobody stopped me.

As a university student it felt a bit awkward to say,

'*Go re ka marketer* (I am looking for a job),' because I thought my standards were higher than that – that a job should be given to me without me even asking. I had thought so for a long time. That is when I discovered that, in this world, there is no entitlement. On campus, I discovered a lot of things. Even though we had all come to university for the same thing – to get an education – our backgrounds and our circumstances showed how desperate we were to get the qualifications we had come for. When I conversed with my fellow students about coursework, or life in general, I could easily sense entitlement from some of them.

I finally got a job in Witbank at Kusile Power Station. The coal-fired power station being constructed by Eskom, the state electricity utility, was in the middle of nowhere. There was nothing neighbouring Kusile, except for the N4 to Pretoria to the west and N12 to Johannesburg to the east. Another power station, Kendal, was fifteen kilometres away. Kusile was the largest construction site in the country.

After securing a job, I remembered, again, the timeless words of Hendrik Verwoerd, that 'there [was] no place for [the African] in the European community above the level of certain forms of labour', and that it was 'of no avail for him to receive a training which has as its aim absorption in the European community'.

I realised that Verwoerd had won. The bastard had succeeded; I was now working as a general worker.

Desperate black, uneducated youths were exactly what Kusile wanted. I got the job through Tshepo Ntlantleng, who transported workers to Kusile. Mr Ntlantleng was acquainted with my sister Akani. He was a very good man. He embraced me and taught me some important virtues when I stayed with him at the compound in Sizanani, Bronkhorstspruit. Unfortunately, we didn't stay together for very long. He took me to the Ndlovu house in Bronkhorstspruit. He would come and pick me up when we went to work, and would drop me off again when our shift was over. I was told that the Ndlovus were businesspeople and were out of the country, so in essence I would be living in and guarding their house.

The house was in Riamar Park, which was previously a whites-only residential area. But things had changed. What I saw there in Bronkhorstspruit were high-class, educated, important black people, living well in their quiet homes, working in big jobs and driving big cars. Those black people had a different attitude from what I knew. They acted as if they were better off than their black brothers down in Zithobeni or Rethabiseng, two townships to the west of Riamar Park, under the impression that they were incomparably decent people. They tried by all means to imitate white people. I know now, of course, that what I was really seeing was a version of those 'successful' black people back in Atteridgeville. The only difference was that the ones in Bronkhorstspruit had been brainwashed even more thoroughly.

There was a tollgate on the N4 road close to Riamar Park to the east. To the north, there was a beautiful golf course towards town. The Ndlovu house was very big, like the one my mother used to work in. It was understandable because they had kids. Siya, their first born, was at school in Pretoria. Hlelo and Mpho were at boarding school in Vereeniging. It was only me and the dog in the house. Captain was his name. Captain reminded me of the dog that had bitten my mother, but I liked him. After work, I would feed him.

But back to Kusile. On my first day, while I was sitting on a bench and waiting, I could see some of the employees getting too excited to see us. In every organisation I had ever been in, I had always seen the existing members feel more powerful. Even on campus, I did not get it when people laughed at the first-year students. We had all been freshers at some point. It was awkward for me, having secured our piece jobs, finding myself in the same queue as a man who was the same age as my father as we prepared to sign our contracts.

As we all anxiously waited on the benches, I remember one young lady, Mpho Sekodi, weeping and saying, 'I should not be working as a general worker. My mother was a general worker. I should be sitting at home like my friend.' I felt sorry for her. But, after a while, I thought about her friend – who insisted that she would not work as a general worker, but did not even have matric. I said to myself, *People with degrees are sitting at home. Who does she think she is?*

The human resources guy kept on asking a bunch of questions. But, funnily enough, it seemed I heard only one: 'How many children do you have?' As expected, everyone had children. These men and women were doing it for their children. I knew this for sure a few

226

weeks later: when we were working on site, I noticed that one guy, Lucas Masongo, had written a different name on his hard hat. When I asked him about the name, he told me that was the name of his three-month-old baby girl. He said he had written it on his hard hat so that, when he put it on, he would remember who he was doing it for. That deeply touched my heart.

Even though I did not have children when I worked at Kusile, I was always thinking about my 'child' back in Johannesburg, which was university, and how I was going to 'support' it, by paying my outstanding tuition fees.

Travelling every day from Bronkhorstspruit to Witbank with Mr Ntlantleng, I would look at Kusile from a distance and see an engineer's imagination coming to life. Looking at the bridges that overlapped one another, and all the machines that were being built on site, I realised the complexity of the human mind. Seeing a crane lift a load of several tons that would have taken hundreds, if not thousands, of men to lift made me realise the progress in technology that we had made since the Stone Age.

I realised that white people have made significant progress in technology, but I started imagining a world in which black people could start ruling and creating. (I know this sounds weird, but, recalling the witchcraft I used to witness at Bevhula, I held out hope that black people would discover a way to make people fly; I'm willing to bet that a granny from our village could beat the Wright brothers. You can laugh all you want, but you never know what will be happening a thousand years from today. Okay, let me stop hallucinating.)

At its completion, Kusile was expected to be the fourth-largest power station in the world. It employed about eighteen thousand people, including the people who worked on the subcontracts. But when the construction projects ended, it would employ only about six hundred permanent employees. The same goes for Kendal, and Medupi, and any other power station in the country. It reminded me of the story of the White House in America – the house had been built by slaves seeking liberty, but they had only now elected the first black man to reside there. A half-black man, if I am allowed to say.

At Kusile, I learnt a lot about what people went through in the workplace. Since my job was a general one, I would pump water, clean the yard, bring the tools for the guys who were erecting the stalls – in short, do everything that was not considered to be a job. But I was very inspired by my colleagues' prayers before the start of a shift, thanking God for the blessing of having a job.

We worked as a unit. Every individual gave one hundred per cent. That is when I realised that the fifty-fifty thing did not work. Even though we spoke different languages, we understood each other through our work. We understood that a chain was as strong as its weakest link. Unfortunately, we had a very strict supervisor. You know those bosses who never want to see anybody sitting down? We knew there was a problem when he spoke only Afrikaans and could speak no English. He failed to understand that everyone was working as hard as he was. I cannot argue that I was still an infant when it came to leadership, but I did learn that it was not about how loud you could scream at people, but how loud your actions screamed. It was about having a vision and leading people to achieve it, inspiring them along the way. Whether you led from the front or from behind did not matter – as long as you reached the destination. Black people are poor because of oppression by white people. That's a fact. So, being oppressed by a white person is one thing. But by a black person? This was like receiving services from a government institution – so much pain for one person to bear.

I would work night shifts to see how it felt to work against nature – to count down the hours relentlessly, anticipating an end of what would be a tough shift in the cold.

I remember one day, while we were working night shift, I was sitting with my colleagues having supper in the canteen. I saw Mpho Sekodi, whom we'd met on our first day. After taking her supper box, she walked past our table and did not greet us. To try to diffuse what could later become tension, I greeted her.

'Why don't you greet us?' I asked her.

'Oh, I didn't see you guys,' she replied, and walked on.

One of the guys I was sitting with turned to me, unimpressed. 'That person clearly saw us,' he shot back. 'Do you know why she did not greet us?'

'No,' I said. 'You will tell me, won't you?'

'It's because we are general workers. If we were some safety officers or supervisors, she would have greeted us.'

I did not want to agree with him, but I could not disagree with him either.

Not only was this part of Kusile much more exciting for me, but I felt more relaxed among people who were being their natural selves and not putting on airs. Although I lived in Riamar Park, my instincts were never to feel that I was better than any other person.

Time and again, I would see the subtle frustrations that a lot of people were struggling with on site. 'These Germans and Americans are just pointing out what we should do. We work like slaves in our own country,' Ephraim Musipha noted. From that day, I started to notice something very odd. I saw that white people in the workplace were more respected than any other groups of people.

I remembered a funny story my uncle once told me. Do you know those 'back in the day' stories that uncles like to tell? He said there was once a retrenchment round at his workplace. The assistant to the managing director, Mr Khumalo, called a meeting to tell the workers the bad news. As expected, there were a lot of quarrels, and it was very hostile. Mr Khumalo told them that they would get a package of five hundred thousand, but they could not accept it. Here is the funny part: when Mr Smith, the managing director, came in, he said the same thing that Mr Khumalo had said. The only difference was that Mr Smith had said, 'You will walk away with a package of half a million.' The workers erupted in cheers. The fear of, or respect for, Mr Smith was greater than for Mr Khumalo.

Some systems haven't changed: what we now have are black faces in government, but white people retaining capital and the total ownership of industries. These whites hear prominent politicians, like the Malemas, doing all the tough talking. Then, they get even angrier with their black employees; some of them go as far as trying to bury us alive, as we saw in the coffin case in Middelburg in 2017.

At Kusile, they were very strict when it came to safety. Everyone was supposed to buckle up while being transported on site. A security guard once found me not wearing my safety belt. The guy threatened to take away my access card. It was the right thing to do, but would lead to my first warning. So, he asked me to buy him a cold drink. Basically, he asked me to pay a bribe. 'You know we earn peanuts here,' he pointed out. I learnt that, if you want to find out about the weaknesses or biases of any organisation, just have a conversation with the security guards at the gate. He had all the qualities of a good traffic officer. I told him that I did not have money – that I was flat broke that month. So, day after day, he would be on my case. I found it very funny that failing to buckle up could cause such an issue. It was like he wanted my whole salary. What he didn't know was that I was also hustling, just like he was.

Occasionally, I would see people getting their first, second or final warning. I saw what that did to a man's confidence. At the end of a shift, I would sleep like a baby. I finally understood why my mother used to go to sleep very early: hard labour is not child's play. As I grew older, I started to realise that some things were not easy.

When my parents would come back with the goodies they bought every day, as a kid I did not know what they had been through. I just saw the reassuring smiles; I did not know the pain of their labour.

But when I was working, I felt like I was living. Maybe that is a good reason why they call working 'making a living' – because it comes with so much pride. When I got paid, I felt at least five metres tall. It was the first time I'd ever had any money to speak of, all my own, in my whole life. The violence of poverty and crime was real. I tried to pay back the university with the pennies I was earning in my new job, but it felt as if I was pouring soil into the ocean with the aim of stabilising the ground: it did not make much difference. But it always pained me to see how my colleagues laboured, like slaves, only to spend it all on alcohol in one weekend or one day.

After payday, I would normally go and buy groceries to carry me through the month. I remember I once went to Shoprite to buy some groceries. While I was queuing there in my dirty overalls, an intelligent black woman – you know, those *mamas* who look like teachers with spectacles and relaxed hair? – looked at me, unimpressed, but never uttered a single word. She gave me that 'Really, at this age?' look. Her stare was contagious, so I ended up staring back at her with that 'What can I do, *mama*?' look. That awkward, non-verbal exchange with a complete stranger reassured me that there were people who still cared about us young people. It was not only that lady: a lot of people at Kusile would ask me why I was not at school. Many people at Kusile were working for their kids. So, it was perplexing for them to see a child working there.

Chapter 25

Zimbabwe: The struggle

In a remarkable turn of events, the Ndlovus came back to visit their home in Riamar Park. I remember the day they came back. I had just come back from a shift, and the electricity had run out. I remember I was very perplexed when I walked into the yard, because I noticed movement in the house. At first, I thought they were criminals, but there was no sign of a burglary. I walked into the house carefully.

Mrs Ndlovu quickly calmed me down. '*Hello, kunjani?* (Hello, how are you?)'

'*Ngiyaphila kunjani?* (I'm good, and you?)' I realised that they could be the owners of the house. 'I guess you are Mrs Ndlovu, right?' I asked nervously.

'Yes, Tshepo told us that there was a new person in our house,' she said, smiling.

Even though it was very dark in the house, I quickly sensed her gracious spirit. We talked a little bit about the electricity issue. I went to the shop to buy a candle, then I introduced myself properly. It turned out they were involved in the mining industry. They had investments in a mine in Zimbabwe.

As I talked to them, I told them that I was a mining

engineering student and I was looking for a mine in which to do my practical training. Mrs Ndlovu then referred me to the managing director, who was also a South African. Zoliswa Mnguni was his name. Mr Mnguni interviewed me. I got to explain my academic background, and he was very impressed. I always carried my certificates that I'd got at school through the years, especially the ones I'd got at UJ, with me. He was clearly not eager to take someone whom he considered dumb to a foreign land.

I succeeded in the interview. A few weeks later, I had acquired a passport and was ready to go to Mugabeland.

I had every happy emotion in my body. I called my mother to tell her the good news. Her reaction was, '*Leswi unga ntima nwananga, uta vuya uri wa njhani kwele?* (Since you are already dark in complexion, you will come back even darker.)'

I didn't care about my mother's brainwashed thoughts – I was just happy because I had finally found a mine, and was going to do my practical training in a foreign land. I had always wanted to get out of South Africa to explore the world; Zimbabwe was a good starting point. The mine was situated in Kadoma.

I thought I was going to board an aeroplane for the first time in my life. Unfortunately, we never flew on my first trip to Zimbabwe. I was a little bit disappointed. A few months later, though, I would fly for the first time to Cape Town on a business trip. Then, my heart was satisfied.

When Mr Mnguni told me that my interview had been

successful, I remembered my father and grandfather who had left Limpopo for Gauteng in search of better opportunities.

We crossed the border at Beit Bridge. I was so shocked to see the bribery that was taking place. We waited for about ten hours before our papers were in order. The police were involved in arranging for illegal immigrants to come into South Africa. I was angry: the police were breaking the law there but, at the opposite end of the spectrum, in places like Hillbrow they were stopping people who looked like me. If they did their job at the border, surely they wouldn't need to walk like hypocrites in the streets of Joburg, searching people? But, in a few minutes' time, I was going to be a foreigner in Zimbabwe, so I kept my emotions in check.

When I arrived there, some Zimbabweans were sceptical about why a South African would come to look for an opportunity in their dry land. I realised that it is only when you put things bigger than yourself on your shoulders that you discover your full potential. I had learnt that, to go the furthest, I needed to be willing to go where others were not willing to go. Mr Mnguni, who had now become my mentor, said to me, 'Clinton, if you want to live an uncommon life, you must do things that are uncommon.'

Mr Mnguni did everything to make sure that I settled well in Zimbabwe. The South African embassy, which was located in the country's capital, Harare, knew about my presence. Mr Mnguni knew all the gurus of Zimbabwe. He was friends with a parliamentarian and other big shots of Kadoma, such as Alfred Moyo and Blessing Kolo.

And he would always introduce me to these guys: 'This is Clinton Chauke. He is our mining engineer in training. In a few months, he is the one who will be running the business,' were his favourite lines.

I was shocked to see the wealth of the people who hung out with Mr Mnguni. It is not a sin to be wealthy and, sure, it is not a curse to lack. But in Zimbabwe it felt a bit awkward to see rich people. It made me realise that one could be among the poor and still be rich. When I looked at my own life, South Africa was considered a rich nation on the continent, but I was living in poverty.

Soon after my arrival, the Ndlovus came back from South Africa and I got to know them better. Mr Mnguni looked more like their son. They had this beautiful parent–child bond that I liked. They respected each other, even when they disagreed. They were elegant.

The Ndlovus were highly intellectual. Mr Ndlovu was a graduate of the University of Cape Town and Mrs Ndlovu was a graduate of the University of Johannesburg. Before she ventured into mining, she had been a teacher. She would always tell me a bunch of stories about her teaching days. We talked about everything. She would open up to me; at times, it was too much for me, because I was very private. I didn't like to talk much about my family. I was embarrassed, most of the time, to talk about my poverty in front of these high achievers. We talked about everything – she even told me that she used to work with the mother of the Orlando Pirates player Happy Jele. Each time I spoke to her, I would learn something new. She was a remarkable person.

When Mr Mnguni was in South Africa, I would be with Mr Ndlovu. Mr Ndlovu was very political. He reminded me of my high school teacher Mr Mathibela. He was really fed up with the political climate in South Africa. He was also interested in the subject of religion. We would have fierce debates about religion, as he taught me how religion had been used to colonise and exploit our people back in South Africa. I would argue, and say we had made progress. Then, he would shoot back, 'Well, Clinton, you have made progress, but do you have land?'

He would paralyse me with such questions. As time went on, I came to appreciate him more and more. He really forced me to think. He engaged me fiercely, as he would his own son. He also stretched my mind to distant horizons. He would even send me videos of documentaries about our history. I became friends with him. He treated me like a son.

I was grateful that I met Mr Ndlovu when I did, because staying with him made me realise one simple thing: that apartheid was founded on the religious ideology – Christianity in particular! – that whites were superior and blacks inferior. 'Slaves, obey your earthly masters . . .' When I analysed this scripture from the Bible, I added one and one, and realised that it made two.

This country did not allow the black man to grow spiritually, socially, politically or economically. It only allowed him to grow physically so he could work for the white man. I know that the things I say will never make it into the Sunday morning sermons at church, but they will certainly make it to the dinner table talks when we are comfortable and surrounded by our loved ones. That's where we become our real selves and open our hearts and accept the truth: South Africa is a fractured country. White people are used to black people working for them – in their offices by sweeping and cleaning, and in their homes by looking after their children and doing the gardening. Black people are used to doing those things for white people. And, when they get to rest on Sunday at church, to both races the clergymen preach that Jesus is happy with this set-up and that, ultimately, Jesus rules the world. This kind of abnormality that has been accepted as normality is what makes it difficult to fix the race problem that we have in this country.

In my opinion, Jesus is currently ruling the world with white people. Yes: white people are currently ruling the world. If we are to be serious about equality, we must first teach the black man that he is worthy of being alive and that he is a complete human being. Sometimes, this is not clear: black people sing an old Sesotho hymn, '*Jo Ke Mohlolohlolo ha ke ratwa lenna*' ('What a miracle it is for someone like me to be loved') at church; they bleach their skins; they buy Brazilian hair; they use Clinton as a first name instead of Wisani; they fake a British or American accent.

I left organised religion and became an agnostic. I avoided being an atheist deliberately because I didn't have the time or energy to debate the existence or non-existence of God. I didn't think it was worth it. I realised that many preachers, through all manner of fake British or American accents, were interested in enriching themselves and promoting their personal agendas about morality and telling people how they should lead their lives, because a lot of people don't know. Many preachers were very satisfied to sell hopes and dreams and aspirations to people who could hardly afford them. They were very far away from solving the economic problems that faced many of our black people. Also, the idea of waiting for some Messiah from Nazareth (over six thousand kilometres away), who would come down from the sky to save me, started to wear thin! However, I was not quick to forget what history has shown us: that when the people are confused and their state has been captured by the Guptas, they tend to look for a saviour. Some find a saviour in political organisations, some in religious organisations, some in taverns, and some – like me – humble ourselves and proudly declare that we don't know where to go.

Breaking with organised religion was the most difficult thing in my life. I had a message for black people. But I've learnt the hard way that black people will not hear a single word from your mouth when you speak about Jesus outside of a religious context. When you tell them that Jesus was a historical figure, just like most great figures of the past, they will immediately pray for you. I still wanted a sense of belonging, though, and I knew I would no longer feel it.

Today, I feel that Christianity is the most evil entity that has ever been invented. To me, telling a man that his problems will be over when he is dead is the greatest sin. Yes, as black people we can find solace in Christianity, but we will never find unity there. Christianity tells people that they are incomplete. It gives them laws that are impossible to uphold, and that contradict one another. It tells you that, whatever you do, you will never be complete, and that you need a saviour. A saviour who is sitting up in the sky – and who is probably white. Come on, don't act dumb. When you imagine God, do you imagine someone dark, like me? No! You imagine this yellow-bone old man sitting in a higher place, surrounded by some more yellow-bones, looking at us going about our stupid business here on earth. What a shame!

This is part of the reason why black people are afraid of white people: in white people, they see the image of God. God have mercy on us. White people, please have mercy on us. Maybe I say this because I am African – a descendant of slaves. Poor Africans, we who read nothing but the book the missionaries gave us. If reading it gave blessings, no one would be more blessed than the blacks. Yet no one takes more hell than the blacks.

When I'm bored on Sundays, I pop into some of the white churches in town. You should see white people's faces when I do: they're priceless. It feels like I'm in heaven, surrounded by those white faces – it's as if I have finally arrived at the place I always dreamt about during worship time at His Rest.

Look, I'm not trying to attribute every evil that Christianity has brought into our communities to the white man. A lot of Africans have acquired wealth and status through the Bible. They own private jets and drive cars that only 'Buffalo' Ramaphosa can afford to be driven around in, and are treated as if they are more important than the so-called Buffalo could ever wish to be. But Christianity's days are numbered. The days of ignorance are numbered. The future of the world is based on reason and logic.

Staying with the Ndlovus made me feel like I was at home. Going to Zimbabwe made me realise that we, as the children of this continent, should be responsible for our own natural resources. With mining being the driving force of our economy, we should really stand up. *We* should get a share what the Germans or the Swiss or the Anglo Americans came here for. As Barack Obama said when he addressed the students at UJ's Soweto campus in 2013: 'So in your lives, there will be time to test your faith. But no matter how old you grow, I say to you today, don't lose those qualities of youth – your imagination, your optimism, your idealism. Because the future of this continent is in your hands'.

Along with the Ndlovus, Mr Mnguni always motivated me. He was genuinely very keen to see me succeed in mining. He had started from humble beginnings and worked his way up to senior management. He travelled all over the world in his career, and knew everything about mining. He was everything I aspired to be in my career. He was a down-to-earth Wits graduate – I know this for sure because you can never have a conversation with a Wits graduate without their telling you about their alma mater. Mr Mnguni may have been extremely intelligent, but he would never show off. The agility of his brain intimidated me.

He would always give a philosophical answer to the simplest of my questions. 'So *Bab' Mnguni,* what do you think *ngama-aliens?* (So, Mr Mnguni, what's your take on aliens?)' I would ask.

'*Uya bona whe Chauke, ama* scientists *athi* there's ninety-nine per cent chance *ukuthi ama* aliens *akhona,* the mystery is how to locate them (Here's the thing, Mr Chauke. The scientists say there's a ninety-nine per cent chance that the aliens exist. The mystery is how to locate them),' he would answer.

I also indicated to him that I didn't like mining, and wanted to be a motivational speaker instead. He replied, 'I also don't like mining, but that's where the money is, bro. You can't be a lizard here and expect to be a crocodile when you leave here. Focus on being a crocodile where you are. Right now, let's focus on you getting the blasting certificate, because that's the most important piece of paper you need right now.'

Seeing how Mr Mnguni's brain worked, I finally agreed that Wits did, indeed, produce great students. He taught me a lot of things I know today about mining that I never learnt in the lecture rooms. He also taught me a lot of life skills. He liked me because I was disciplined: I didn't smoke or drink.

Our mine was not as big as the one in Syferfontein, but the conditions there were the same. On my days off, which were mostly on weekends, Martin Wilson, a production manager at the mine, would take me to the neighbouring areas. Martin was born and bred in Zimbabwe, so he knew all the corners. He would take me to places like Brompton. There, I would watch small kids 'korokozing' – mining illegally. When I talked to them, they told me that if they did not work, they would starve. School was not important to them, because there were no industries in their area, so mining was their best option. It broke my heart to see child labour and teenage pregnancy being the norm, young people growing up with no prospects for the future.

Seeing that kind of poverty made me realise that I was, in fact, richer. You could never know how poor you were until you had seen what wealth looks like. And you could never know how rich you were until you knew what poverty was. In South Africa, when you were not happy about something, you protested. In Zimbabwe, when you were not happy about something, you went to work – even if you were a baby.

Observing these small but powerful truths made me upset. I was there on my own, far away from my family and friends. I could not tell anyone, so I kept it to myself. I realised that, when I was uncomfortable, I grew. I got to know myself better when I was in despair. Seeing the trials and tribulations of those kids helped me to grow.

The only problem I had in Zimbabwe was the language. I had to learn the language very quickly. I realised that it was no longer as easy to learn a new language as it had been when I moved back to Pretoria – it is a bit difficult to learn a new language when you are older. I remember I once got into a bus that was going to Gweru. I spoke English to the bus conductor. He looked at me from my toes to my forehead, then shrugged and walked away. He couldn't comprehend why a dark-skinned Zimbabwean would speak English to him. He gave me that 'just be yourself' look. It was painful: I honestly couldn't speak chiShona.

So, I started to learn chiShona by listening to the music of the likes of Leonard Dembo and the legendary Oliver Mtukudzi, and watching more speeches that President Robert Mugabe had made on YouTube. I remember stumbling upon a speech in which Mugabe said that 'South Africans will kick down a statue of a dead white man but won't even attempt to slap a live one. Yet they can stone to death a black man simply because he's a foreigner'.

I remembered the guys at home, then just laughed it off.

As the days went on, I started to understand chiShona. It was a bit similar to Tshivenda, which was an advantage for me – I could speak Tshivenda.

Another thing I found challenging was trading in US dollars. One dollar had much more value than one rand, but in my mind I always thought it was equivalent to one rand. As a result, I was very careless with my money. I later figured out that I could buy a lot of things with one dollar, even though my mind could not comprehend it well.

While I was in Zimbabwe, the only grandparent I had known – the grandparent who had rescued me earlier in my life – passed away. I was forced to go back home and pay my respects. I found that the distance between Elim and Musina was very small. Elim was very close to Zimbabwe, in ways I never imagined.

I had a good time when I visited places like Bulawayo, because there were a lot of Ndebeles there. I would speak to them in Ndebele. As soon as they heard that I was from South Africa, they would be happy. They assumed everyone from South Africa had money. People were welcoming, had smiles on their faces, and were always willing to talk to me. I found it very refreshing to be among people who loved me. I was shown incredible kindness and understanding, and was never questioned about my presence or purpose there.

I then thought about how we treated Zimbabweans in South Africa. I imagined how I would have coped if they had returned this favour – if they called me bad names and said I was taking their jobs. Of course, they would be right.

A few months later, when I was reflecting on the improbable journey that had taken me to Zimbabwe, I realised the importance of taking action in the face of the unknown. Had I sat at home like that lady who'd said she didn't want to be a general worker, I would not have had the privilege of living in a foreign country, or the opportunity to learn a foreign language. Or the chance to trade in US dollars.

Chapter 26:

I will never vote

With all the experiences I'd had got in the first two decades of our democracy, I had lost faith in all our leaders. As a result, I had told myself that I was no longer going to vote. I was aware that I did not have to protest or be shot in the back for my rights . . . people had already done that for me. All I had to do was to take my smart ID and go to the polls.

Every time I reiterated my decision in front of my mother, she became disappointed with me. My mother loved the ANC. She loved Nelson Mandela, for obvious reasons. She also loved Thabo Mbeki. My mother loved Thabo Mbeki simply because he gave us social grants. And when Jacob Zuma assumed office, my mother loved President Zuma, despite all the allegations against him – because he gave us grants as well. What's more, President Zuma had extended the age for receiving grants to eighteen. So, despite the rape charges and corruption charges, President Zuma was a good man. He was also a good man to me: without his help, my life would have been miserable.

This was true of a lot of people from my mother's generation.

I knew that, in a democracy as strong as our own, it was very important to vote. My vote was important; young people's votes were crucial for making sure that our democracy functioned well. Mostly, when people were given a chance to vote, they voted for peace rather than war. They voted for the good things.

The decision I had made not to vote was wrong. I was even disappointed in myself. But I looked at my options: the three biggest parties in the country.

Take the Economic Freedom Fighters (EFF). Although I liked their argument for change, I could not vote for them. They had brilliant, educated, young minds, but their track record was not something I wanted to associate myself with. The seed upon which the party had been established was not appetising. Their policies were good, but their approach was always hostile. When I went to the polls, I would carry my ID card, but I would not forget that I was an African child. I could not elect someone who did not embody the characteristics of an African child: respect and dignity. Overall, I think, that is the reason why the EFF has not been able to garner a lot of support.

To be fair, however, I have to admit that it was Julius Malema's politics and rhetoric that had awoken my political conscience – and that of many people of my age. Whether you thought Julius was stupid or not, you could feel his presence throughout the country. Before him, Parliament had been just a secluded place where the old and educated met and discussed some important things, and somehow excluded us. I learnt to listen to him, and realised that his cry was the same as mine. He was also a young black man who felt that his land had been stolen from him. All the other stuff – the shouts of 'Shoot the farmer!' and 'Kill the boer!' – was incidental to that cry. But I personally decided that the political programme that Juju had forged for himself and his friends would never be incidental to my own cry. No vote for Juju.

I then looked at the Democratic Alliance (DA). The party had a long history of racial tension. But, to its credit, it had really tried to heal those wounds. Honestly, I had not really given myself time to look at their policies, because I was always looking at how they dealt with race relations. When I walked into Parliament and looked in their section, I only saw white people. The only black person I saw was sitting at the front: the party's leader. First it was Lindiwe Mazibuko, and then came Mmusi Maimane. I then thought: if one eloquent and smart black person was going to be used as an instrument for getting votes at every election, we have a problem. I could not put such a party in power.

Finally, I took a closer look at the African National Congress (ANC). The party was a shadow of its former self. The ANC of Winnie Madikizela-Mandela, the ANC of Walter Sisulu, the ANC of Oliver Tambo, the ANC that our grandparents were proud of, was long gone. That pride was substituted by a leadership that was greedy – a leadership that was full of hungry people. A leadership that had only one mandate: personal gain first, and the people second. The notion that the ANC would rule until Jesus came back had made its leaders more arrogant than ever, believing that they would never be over-thrown. I could not vote for that which was autocratic and corrupt. The leadership of Jacob Zuma was a complete failure. I don't care about the grants that we used to get – after all, that was taxpayers' money. I was fed up with the ANC. Even when my mother's homeboy, Cyril (a Muvenda man born in Chiawelo), won the ANC presidency, I was not moved at all: all the top six leaders were from the age of President Zuma, and were even more dangerous. I have a feeling that Mr Ramaphosa will never get anything done; he will only become more like his top six comrades.

Today, I am not a big fan of the Buffalo, but I won't lie – when Cyril became president, I too had hope. In his State of the Nation speech, he said nothing new, just the same things that were said at the first Consultative Conference of the ANC held in Morogoro, Tanzania, in 1969. But he did inspire the nation, especially by quoting Bra Hugh's words, 'send me'. Zuma had set the bar so low that even I was tempted to believe a politician. But nice speeches won't make a 'better life for all'. Delivering services will. I want to give Cyril a chance, but I resist giving him my full support. He is a politician, a very skilful one. He will always serve his own interests above those of the people – you are on your own, homie!

Because of corruption, the country had a deficit of billions of rands when he came to power. To remedy this, the government increased VAT for the first time since I was born. This made the people very angry, especially the poor. Days after Malusi Gigaba increased the VAT rate, he was reshuffled, moving back into his old portfolio of forging IDs and stuff like that. Bathabile Dlamini was made minister of women, a very big – and unfunny – joke to the beloved women of South Africa. DD Mabuza was made deputy president. I have no comment here: since I am still a temporary resident of Mpumalanga, I want to enjoy my time out here. Fikile Mbalula was left out of Cabinet, which put the future of black Twitter in jeopardy, because no one captured the very essence of South African politics – which is entertainment and jokes – like he did. Poor Mbaks!

In essence, what I'm trying to say is, Ramaphosa and Zuma: same WhatsApp group!

I always tried to tell my friends my opinion when I would see a lady with three kids, for example, all from different fathers. I told them not to call her a slut. I would always ask them: have you ever realised how high your hopes are raised during the election season? Have you seen how you get promised RDP houses? How you are promised jobs? Have you counted the number of parks that get built around that time? Even though you knew that you had been screwed many times, you could not help expecting better this time around. I reminded them that they were no different from that lady. We were the sluts, with the politicians screwing us over and over!

I may have been too young to understand what was really going on in this country, but I was not too young to recognise that something was wrong and that change was needed.

I just did not know how to confront it.

So, until there was a significant change in those political parties, I would not exercise my right to vote. I had no time for a government that would crush people and then punish them for not being able to stand up under its weight.

This thinking had made me reluctant, even on campus, to vote for any of the parties. I saw brilliant leaders there, who were not disrespectful or racist or corrupt, but a vote for either party on campus would imply support for them on the national level. Although I had a close relationship with the SRC guys, I was always suspicious of them – especially the ones who started their sentences with, 'Eh chief.' You would find that most of those guys, who were in the student body, had been enrolled for over seven years. I know that degrees are not easy to get, but I would ask tough questions as well. Those SRC guys, I would always find them drinking and hosting parties to which they had invited celebrities. I would see them at the beginning of a semester, campaigning and asking for votes. But I would never see them come back and ask how they could assist the students who could not afford to pay their tuition fees, or those who did not have food.

I applauded them for fighting for us when we got academic exclusions, but I felt they should have widened their leadership. Driving a Polo and impressing a few girls on campus was one thing. But, at the end of the day, what were they were saying to the student who came to class on an empty stomach? To the student who was struggling to secure practical training? Or to a student who came from an impoverished background, like me, but was failing his or her modules? Nobody fought for those students. Without anybody fighting for them, they lost the battles they tried to fight for themselves.

The SRC guys were not aware of their power. I believed that one tiny voice – the voice of the president of the SRC – could have changed a department. If it could change the department, it could change the faculty. If it could change the faculty, it could change the campus. If it could change the campus, it could change the university. If it could change the university, then it could change the entire country.

When the country celebrated Freedom Day, I would no longer go to the Union Buildings to celebrate there like I used to with my father when I was very young. Instead, I took the time to reflect on how far we had travelled as a country.

When we used to go to the Union Buildings with my father, after President Zuma's speech I would watch live performances by popular musicians such as Malaika, Chomee, Mafikizolo, Spikiri and other big names, and I would be so glad. But, as I grew up, I observed days like these being hijacked by our politicians. I then thought, if we took days like those and turned them into political rallies, we were only robbing ourselves of time to reflect on how long we had travelled and how far we still needed to go as a country.

On 27 April 1994, I knew for sure that I was in my mother's womb – I was born in September. But I did not know what was happening in the country, or even the world. I was still being fed by an umbilical cord. Not mature enough to go out into the world. In a sense, I was not free. So, every time we celebrated the day, I asked myself a few questions: Am I free today? Am I mature today? Do I still depend on my mother? Am I ready to go into the world? These were not easy questions, but I would just leave them to my fellow young people – my fellow born-frees. This word, 'born-free', weighed heavy on my conscience, by the way. It implied one thing, while it failed to highlight another. Democratic South Africa had only brought political freedom; socioeconomic freedom remained a myth.

Sometimes, I would get frustrated and feel that, if my grandfather had not gone to Johannesburg, but into exile, somehow I would have been competent for some of the occupations in this country. It looked like going to exile had been a qualification in itself in this country. I admired all those people who had fought and bled and died for this country. I admired their patriotism. But, at the same time, I could not underscore the fact enough that there were also patriots in this country who had not fought physical battles. I believed we were all patriots. The minute somebody tried to prove to me that he or she was more patriotic than I was, the whole point of patriotism was lost.

Whenever I tried to measure the maturity of our de-mocracy, I was always tempted to compare it to a twenty-two-year-old. This was a very complex comparison. I could think of a twenty-two-year-old who was as mature as a twenty-two-year-old, a twenty-two-year-old who was as mature as a thirty-two-year-old, or, the worst-case scenario, a twenty-two-year-old who was as mature as a twelve-year-old. So, I could not draw a proper conclusion. I did note that our democracy was old enough to drink. Maybe we needed that drink after all, I thought. At over twenty-one, our democracy was legally an adult. A young adult, but an adult nonetheless.

Many people believed that voting for politicians was important, and that every person should participate in elections. They believed that not voting was against Ubuntu (humanity), that those who choose not to vote don't really care about the well-being of society. But walking around Mshongo was motivation enough for me to stay at home and mind my own business. I did not believe that any of the parties could change anything. And, by rejecting voting for the politicians, I was honouring my hero, Steve Biko, who refused to accept the 'working within the system' theory. So, I would rather die working in the mines than rallying behind politicians who are controlled by white capitalists: politicians who don't give a damn about my parents in Mshongo, or my cousin in a wheelchair, or my grandmother in Bevhula, or some of my friends who are still busy with their studies at UJ.

Chapter 27
Maybe South Africa
will change

Despite all the solid evidence of the inequalities that still existed in our country, I did not think that blaming apartheid would do us any justice. I remember, once, walking the streets of the rich suburb of Hatfield, Pretoria, with my friends, as usual, admiring the houses and the quality of life. Success Nobela asked, 'Why are we living in the squatter camps, though?' Instantly, I laughed at the question. But, as it sunk in, I stopped laughing and started to think how I would answer him.

I could not.

It was very easy for us young, black South Africans to say that our land had been stolen from us (indeed, it had been) and that it was time to take it back, but I strongly believed that you had to know why things were as they were before you developed a plan for fixing them.

I had learnt that, in a democracy as big as ours, to make it work you had to give it time. Getting the land back without knowing how to use it was not an ideal plan, for me. And, after spending some time in Zimbabwe, I could see that it was good that they had got the land back – but they were poor. My friend Brian Moyo told me something that pained me while I was in

Zimbabwe. 'You know, Clinton,' he said, 'we are hungry free men.'

Now that Mugabe has resigned, I feel like Zimbabwe will become more like South Africa. Colonisers will flock to that country to exploit its mineral wealth. But maybe the sad part is that Zimbabwe is living proof that black people are unable to use the land by themselves – or maybe those people are still mentally colonised, and can't, therefore, use the land by themselves?

I understood the cry of my fellow young people regarding the sensitive topic of land. Sure, our cynicism and complaints could be helpful, at times. If we did not question things, we would easily fall into the trap of settling for the least we deserved. But, personally, I felt that the time for blaming apartheid had surely passed. It was time for us to roll up our sleeves and begin a journey of shaping South Africa. I believed that we *had* come a long way as a country. As much as I had changed since I was born, so had our democracy.

I know some people may be annoyed by my empty optimism and may even ask, 'Where are you now? What are you doing? Did you just win the lotto?' As you can imagine, it is impossible to leave the shacks after working for just a few months. Right now, I am living in a rented apartment in downtown Middelburg, close to where I work. Every day, I deal with the small matters of paying the rent, paying the instalment on my little car, and insuring it. As you can imagine, I am still paying black tax, too. And Lucas was right: if I get fired from this job, all these things will be returned to their rightful owners, and my fake middle-class life will be over before it even starts.

If this book does well, after a few months, people will put me up in fancy hotels and on expensive planes, and I will be living the life. But even then, after a while, I will have to go back to the 'hood – Mshongo, the place of so many childhood memories, friends, family, and even my parents. Yes, my parents still stay in Mshongo! I will visit His Rest church. The pastors will pray for me and ask me to repent about everything I said about Jesus in this book. My Tswana friends will ask me whether we are still friends. My Tswana girlfriend might threaten to dump me. I will visit my sister in Soshanguve, who will advise me to say nice things about white people when-ever I appear on TV or radio. I will visit my favourite people, the Ndlovus in Bronkhorstspruit, and tell them about my plans to leave my current job. I will sit there, in front of their big, flat-screen TV, and listen to them telling me that I should be realistic. Occasionally, I will have to visit my extended family in Shirley village and also go to Bevhula village, where I will ultimately be buried.

When I'm dead, my corpse will still endure the pain of travelling over those potholes. I will still struggle, even after my soul has drifted into some unknowable place.

You see, I was born in chains – and, even though I can solve my personal problems through my individual ini-tiatives, I will probably die in chains.

There is still work to be done in this country. Every

one of us, young and old, has a role to play in this democracy to make our land a better nation.

True reconstruction needs to happen first: when a black man himself understands the importance of going into business. Not only that, but also of supporting black businesses. The focus should be on creating, instead of taking and giving. The blacks must use their talents, pull in their education, pull in their technical know-how, and do something for their people. Unless we do that, we will never know what heaven looks like.

Secondly, when the white man accepts that the country's current wealth distribution is not sustainable in the long run, it is up to the white minority to extend the hand of reconciliation. Honestly, we have forgiven them – they gave us Jesus, anyway – but they haven't forgiven us, let alone acknowledged the evil of the past. White people love and admire fighters: just look at how they admire Paul Kruger, but they don't give a damn about Jesus. Some of them are not even aware of this fact.

White people have a problem, and their problem is racism.

Affirmative action is still vital for achieving true reconciliation, but it's sad that a person's skin colour is a criterion for getting a job or reaching a managerial position. Okay, let me just get this out of the way. The fact that I have hatred towards white people collectively as a race, but not on an individual basis, is well understood. And the fact that I have love towards black people in a similar fashion is obvious. I don't think any black person who has studied the black/white race problem can truly love white people, in the same way that any person who has studied Christianity, and has been serious about doing so, can remain truly a Christian.

But, most of the time, I question my emotions about both races. Do I really hate white people, or do I hate the fact that they are more civilised than me? Do I hate white people, or the fact that they apply their minds and work harder than me? Let me put it this way: do I hate black people, or the fact that they are behind in civilisation? Or is the most important question, do I love black people because I am black? In trying to answer all these questions, I think I arrive at having more respect for white people, because everything about me is white, except for my black and beautiful skin. The way I dress is white, the way I speak is white – sometimes, when I speak, I sound more like a white guy. But who can blame me? The black people? No, they cannot blame me, because when I speak Shangaan, they immediately laugh at me and ridicule my mother tongue. They only listen to me when I speak the Queen's English.

When I try to analyse these things, all these confusions, I realise that I have come from defeat. Firstly, as a Shangaan, no matter how tough I am trying to act in this book, I am inferior – when I look at my history, I was defeated in war. Secondly, when I look at my history as a black person, I was also defeated in war. That's why I am inferior, a slave. Bleaching my skin, faking an accent and worshipping Jesus is the result of all this.

Defeat brings so much shame. When two men fight on the street, the one who loses will never have power. Even his children will be despised. That is why, when I walk around the streets of Pretoria today and see the statues of Paul Kruger and company, I don't react. In fact, I am more amused when I see young blacks trying to destroy the statues of those white men. What these young blacks are trying to do is defeat men who have already won that street fight, which is impossible. What I think these young blacks (oh, wait a minute – I am still black, even though I said I am white) – what I think *we* young blacks must do is try to accept the reality that we have, indeed, been defeated – and that, as children of the defeated, we must humble ourselves, and try to consolidate power with the children of the victors, and teach one another to live together, and forget that fight our forefathers had in the street.

This is why I think Mandela was great when he sold us the idea of a rainbow nation. But we black people were very quick to call him a sellout – we didn't want to accept that we had been defeated. I understand this; no one really wants to accept defeat. There is a story I haven't shared in this book yet, about a fight I once had with a little boy at Masizane Primary School. This boy whipped my ass so badly that I didn't write about it when I was describing my experiences in primary school earlier. You see, that is what defeat does: it brings so much shame that you can never put a spotlight on it.

It's going to take time for the black-and-white problem to be fixed. You can see it in small things: in offices, we battle with air conditioning. The whites love cool air, so we, the blacks, must suffer the cold because of their

European tendencies. I propose the decolonisation of air conditioning in the workplace. I think Juju will support me on this one.

Having said all this, is my anger as a born-free justified? No. Anger can never be justified. Anger will only consume you, just like it consumed me when I ruined my date with Basani or when I blame politicians and pastors (which I don't regret, by the way). I don't think blaming apartheid is an option for me. When I look at my mom or my dad, I realise that *they* are the folks who should have complained about apartheid. But they did not. They woke up every day and went to look after somebody else's child, cleaned somebody else's house, did gardening in somebody else's yard. With the little they got from those frustrating activities, they fed their family. They did all of that without complaining. Most of the time, I felt sorry for them because they couldn't spoil their children. My parents wanted to go to school, but unfortunately they were born before Mandela came into office.

I've started to realise that the problems we face are neither black, nor white nor coloured, but problems *people* face – problems people could overcome.

At the end of the day, we all want good things, whether we are black or white or anything in between. We all want to live a nice life. We all want to live in a nice neighbourhood, get the best education, have access to the best health care. We all want to take care of our families – and that's what this is all about.

The likes of Sisulu and Mandela started 'the long walk

to freedom', a journey that is not finished. The walk to freedom may be long, but if we keep on walking, each generation doing its part, I believe we will reach our destination. If my generation, the first generation to walk free, could walk its distance, and the generation of my children could walk its distance, too, then surely my grandchildren will get closer to the destination.

I've become optimistic – not because I think I have all the answers, but because I believe in a better future. Some have suggested that I am a young man filled with hope and vigour, protected by the university's walls. They are probably right. But I remember what the American Robert F. Kennedy said when he addressed students at UCT in 1966: 'This world demands the qualities of youth; not a time of life but a state of mind, a temper of the will, a quality of the imagination, a predominance of courage over timidity, of the appetite for adventure over the life of ease.' So, ultimately, this world needs my inexperience. And, if I could arm myself with education, I could practise all the virtues outlined by the American.

Every time I've felt discouraged or wanted to give up, the class of 1976 has whispered in my ear. Those students still have a story to tell me, as do the sixty-nine fallen heroes of the Sharpeville massacre who still scream from a distance. They tell me that the young people who are willing to change this country can, actually, change it. They must have known what happened to Hector Pieterson that morning, 16 June. Common sense would have told them to go home. But they chose to protest anyway.

I may be frustrated, but I have not given up on this country – the country I love, the country that did so much, systemically, to make sure that my young life was a living hell. But it is this country that has allowed me to study in the same room with an Indian, a coloured and a white student. It is this country that has prevented me from being forced to give up my seat for somebody else on public transport. It is this country that has restored my dignity by removing the signs saying 'Whites Only'.

In Auditorium 1102, Perskor building, on the University of Johannesburg's Doornfontein campus, there I sat – in front of Tarik Habib, an Indian student; with Hendrik de Klerk, a white Afrikaner, on my left; Keagan Pienaar, a coloured student, on my right; and, in front of us, Mr Ndiweni, a black man, giving all of us a lecture.

A milestone, here: twenty years ago, Mr Ndiweni would not even have been allowed to work in the student centre on this campus.

A testament to this country.

Acknowledgements

First and foremost, I would like to thank my parents, Khensani Baloyi and Hlengani Chauke, for giving me the gift of life and for their efforts in making sure that I grew up amidst all the hardships we faced. *Ndza khensa vatswari va mina* (I thank you, my parents).

I thank my two sisters, Tsakani Chauke-Ndlovu and Akani Chauke, for all the memories you gave me growing up and the support that you continue to give me. My love for you both is beyond measure.

To my genius mentor Xolani Gumede, thank you, sir, for teaching me all about life.

To Tshepo Ntlatleng, Baby Mahlangu, and Daniel and Nonhlanhla Ndlovu, thank you for assuming the role of my parents in the bush.

To my fallen heroes – Pastor David Khoza, my high school teacher Jabulani Mathibela, and my grandmother Lettie Baloyi – I know that your ghosts are smiling in the grave.

To my friends Livewell Chauke, Lebogang Maphuthuma, Muhluri Shirinda, Charmaine Valoi, Letlhogonolo Mola, Risima Khosa, Kamogelo Makeketlane, Katlego Ngobeni, and my best friend Success Nobela, thank you, guys, for all the contributions you have made to my life.

To Monique Mathebula, thank you for making me a man.

I thank Sophy Kohler for discovering my manuscript in its early stages and believing that we could make something of it.

I also thank Katlego Ndlovu and my brother-in-law Saddam Ndlovu for pushing me to finish this book. Without you guys, this book wouldn't have been completed.

I thank everyone at the company I currently work for, Solar Mining Services, a member of Solar Industries.

I thank my publisher, Jeremy Boraine, for his wisdom and professionalism, and my editor, Caren van Houwelingen, for her gracious spirit throughout the sleepless nights and hectic deadlines.

Finally, I would like to thank the entire team at Jonathan Ball Publishers down in Cape Town for giving me a voice.

Sources

Maluleke, Tinyiko. Africa's opium is the religion of others, *Mail & Guardian*, 2 April 2015, https://mg.co.za/article/2015-04-01-africas-opium-is-the-religion-of-others, accessed 9 March 2018.

NPR Music. Jay-Z: The Fresh Air Interview, 16 November 2010, https://www.npr.org/2010/11/16/131334322/the-fresh-air-interview-jay-z-decoded, accessed 9 March 2018.

Politicsweb. Hendrik Verwoerd: 10 quotes, 20 September 2016, http://www.politicsweb.co.za/documents/hendrik-verwoerd-10-quotes, accessed 9 March 2018.

Shivambu, Ntsako. Vuwani – the repeat of 1979 (history of Tsonga-Venḓa power struggles), 8 May 2016, https://www.vivmag.co.za/archives/10552/2, accessed 9 March 2018.

South African History Online (n.d.). The June 16 Soweto Youth Uprising, 13 June 2017, http://www.sahistory.org.za/topic/june-16-soweto-youth-uprising, accessed 9 March 2018.

South African History Online (n.d.). 'The spirit of Bandung', Statement by Oliver Tambo to the International Conference in support of the liberation movements of Southern Africa and in Support of the Frontline States, Lusaka, 10 April 1979, http://www.sahistory.org.za/archive/spirit-bandung-statement-oliver-tambo-international-conference-support-liberation-movements-, accessed 9 March 2018.

South African History Online (n.d.). Robert Kennedy, American politician, speaks at the University of Cape Town about the racial inequality of apartheid, 16 March 2011, http://www.sahistory.org.za/dated-event/robert-kennedy-american-politician-speaks-university-cape-town-about-racial-inequality-a, accessed 9 March 2018.